More great books from Veloce …

Rally Giants Series
Audi Quattro (Robson)
Austin Healey 100-6 & 3000 (Robson)
Fiat 131 Abarth (Robson)
Ford Escort MkI (Robson)
Ford Escort RS Cosworth & World Rally Car (Robson)
Ford Escort RS1800 (Robson)
Lancia Delta 4WD/Integrale (Robson)
Lancia Stratos (Robson)
Mini Cooper/Mini Cooper S (Robson)
Peugeot 205 T16 (Robson)
Saab 96 & V4 (Robson)
Subaru Impreza (Robson)
Toyota Celica GT4 (Robson)

General
1½-litre GP Racing 1961-1965 (Whitelock)
AC Two-litre Saloons & Buckland Sportscars (Archibald)
Alfa Romeo 155/156/147 Competition Touring Cars (Collins)
Alfa Tipo 33 (McDonough & Collins)
Alpine & Renault – The Development of the Revolutionary Turbo F1 Car 1968 to 1979 (Smith)
Alpine & Renault – The Sports Prototypes 1963 to 1969 (Smith)
Alpine & Renault – The Sports Prototypes 1973 to 1978 (Smith)
Anatomy of the Works Minis (Moylan)
Armstrong-Siddeley (Smith)
Art Deco and British Car Design (Down)
Autodrome (Collins & Ireland)
Bahamas Speed Weeks, The (O'Neil)
Bluebird CN7 (Stevens)
BMC Competitions Department Secrets (Turner, Chambers & Browning)
British at Indianapolis, The (Wagstaff)
BRM – A Mechanic's Tale (Salmon)
BRM V16 (Ludvigsen)
Bugatti – The eight-cylinder Touring Cars 1920-34 (Price & Arbey)
Bugatti Type 40 (Price)
Bugatti 46/50 Updated Edition (Price & Arbey)
Bugatti T44 & T49 (Price & Arbey)
Bugatti 57 2nd Edition (Price)
Bugatti Type 57 Grand Prix – A Celebration (Tomlinson)
Carrera Panamericana, La (Tipler)
Car-tastrophes – 80 automotive atrocities from the past 20 years (Honest John, Fowler)
Citroën DS (Bobbitt)
Classic British Car Electrical Systems (Astley)
Classic Engines, Modern Fuel: The Problems, the Solutions (Ireland)
Cobra – The Real Thing! (Legate)
Cobra, The last Shelby – My times with Carroll Shelby (Theodore)
Competition Car Aerodynamics 3rd Edition (McBeath)
Competition Car Composites A Practical Handbook (Revised 2nd Edition) (McBeath)
Concept Cars, How to illustrate and design – New 2nd Edition (Dewey)
Cortina – Ford's Bestseller (Robson)
Cosworth – The Search for Power (6th edition) (Robson)
Coventry Climax Racing Engines (Hammill)
Daily Mirror 1970 World Cup Rally 40, The (Robson)
Daimler SP250 New Edition (Long)
Datsun Fairlady Roadster to 280ZX – The Z-Car Story (Long)
Dino – The V6 Ferrari (Long)
Driven – An Elegy to Cars, Roads & Motorsport (Aston)
Fast Ladies – Female Racing Drivers 1888 to 1970 (Bouzanquet)
Ferrari 288 GTO, The Book of the (Sackey)
Ferrari 333 SP (O'Neil)
Fiat & Abarth 124 Spider & Coupé (Tipler)
Fiat & Abarth 500 & 600 – 2nd Edition (Bobbitt)
Fiat in Motorsport
Fiats, Great Small (Ward)
Ford Cleveland 335-Series V8 engine 1970 to 1982 – The Essential Source Book (Hammill)
Ford Focus WRC (Robson)
Ford GT – Then, and Now (Streather)
Ford GT40 (Legate)
Ford Small Block V8 Racing Engines 1962-1970 – The Essential Source Book (Hammill)
Ford versus Ferrari – The battle for supremacy at Le Mans 1966 (Starkey)
Formula 1 - The Knowledge 2nd Edition (Hayhoe)
Formula 1 All The Races - The First 1000 (Smith)
Formula One – The Real Score? (Harvey)
Formula 5000 Motor Racing, Back then ... and back now (Lawson)
The Good, the Mad and the Ugly ... not to mention Jeremy Clarkson (Dron)
Grand Prix Ferrari – The Years of Enzo Ferrari's Power, 1948-1980 (Pritchard)
Grand Prix Ford – DFV-powered Formula 1 Cars (Robson)
Great British Rally, The (Robson)
GT – The World's Best GT Cars 1953-73 (Dawson)
Hillclimbing & Sprinting – The Essential Manual (Short & Wilkinson)
Honda S2000, The Book of The (Long)
Immortal Austin Seven (Morgan)
India – The Shimmering Dream (Reisch/Falls (translator))
Inside the Rolls-Royce & Bentley Styling Department – 1971 to 2001 (Hull)
Intermeccanica – The Story of the Prancing Bull (McCredie & Reisner)
Jaguar - All the Cars (4th Edition) (Thorley)
Jaguar E-type Factory and Private Competition Cars (Griffiths)
The Jowett Jupiter – The car that leaped to fame (Nankivell)
Karmann-Ghia Coupé & Convertible (Bobbitt)
Kris Meeke – Intercontinental Rally Challenge Champion (McBride)
KTM X-Bow (Pathmanathan)
Lamborghini Miura Bible, The (Sackey)
Lamborghini Murciélago, The book of the (Pathmanathan)
Lamborghini Urraco, The Book of the (Landsem)
Lancia 037 (Collins)
Lancia Delta HF Integrale (Blaettel & Wagner)
Lancia Delta Integrale (Collins)
Le Mans Panoramic (Ireland)
Lexus Story, The (Long)
Lola – The Illustrated History (1957-1977) (Starkey)
Lola – All the Sports Racing & Single-seater Racing Cars 1978-1997 (Starkey)
Lola T70 – The Racing History & Individual Chassis Record – 4th Edition (Starkey)
Lotus 18 Colin Chapman's U-turn (Whitelock)
Lotus 49 (Oliver)
Lotus Elan and +2 Source Book (Vale)
Maserati 250F In Focus (Pritchard)
MGA (Price Williams)
MGB & MGB GT– Expert Guide (Auto-doc Series) (Williams)
MGB Electrical Systems Updated & Revised Edition (Astley)
MGB – The Illustrated History, Updated Fourth Edition (Wood & Burrell)
The MGC GTS Lightweights (Morys)
Mitsubishi Lancer Evo, The Road Car & WRC Story (Long)
Montlhéry, The Story of the Paris Autodrome (Boddy)
Motor Racing – Reflections of a Lost Era (Carter)
Motor Racing – The Pursuit of Victory 1930-1962 (Carter)
Motor Racing – The Pursuit of Victory 1963-1972 (Wyatt/Sears)
Motor Racing Heroes – The Stories of 100 Greats (Newman)
Motorsport In colour, 1950s (Wainwright)
Nissan GT-R Supercar: Born to race (Gorodji)]
Nissan – The GTP & Group C Racecars 1984-1993 (Starkey)
Porsche Racing Cars – 1953 to 1975 (Long)
Porsche Racing Cars – 1976 to 2005 (Long)
Porsche – The Rally Story (Meredith)
Powered by Porsche (Smith)
RAC Rally Action! (Gardiner)
Racing Camaros (Holmes)
Racing Colours – Motor Racing Compositions 1908-2009 (Newman)
Racing Mustangs – An International Photographic History 1964-1986 (Holmes)
Rallye Sport Fords: The Inside Story (Moreton)
Runways & Racers (O'Neil)
RX-7 – Mazda's Rotary Engine Sports car (Updated & Revised New Edition) (Long)
Sauber-Mercedes – The Group C Racecars 1985-1991 (Starkey)
SM – Citroën's Maserati-engined Supercar (Long & Claverol)
Speedway – Auto racing's ghost tracks (Collins & Ireland)
Standard Motor Company, The Book of the (Robson)
Steve Hole's Kit Car Cornucopia – Cars, Companies, Stories, Facts & Figures: the UK's kit car scene since 1949 (Hole)
Subaru Impreza: The Road Car And WRC Story (Long)
Supercar, How to Build your own (Thompson)
Tales from the Toolbox (Oliver)
Tatra – The Legacy of Hans Ledwinka, Updated & Enlarged Collector's Edition of 1500 copies (Margolius & Henry)
This Day in Automotive History (Corey)
To Boldly Go – twenty six vehicle designs that dared to be different (Hull)
Toleman Story, The (Hilton)
Toyota Celica & Supra, The Book of Toyota's Sports Coupés (Long)
Toyota MR2 Coupés & Spyders (Long)
Triumph & Standard Cars 1945 to 1984 (Warrington)
Triumph Cars – The Complete Story (new 3rd edition) (Robson)
Triumph TR6 (Kimberley)
Two Summers – The Mercedes-Benz W196R Racing Car (Ackerson)
TWR Story, The – Group A (Hughes & Scott)
TWR's Le Mans Winning Jaguars (Starkey)
Unraced (Collins)
Volvo Estate, The (Hollebone)
You & Your Jaguar XK8/XKR – Buying, Enjoying, Maintaining, Modifying – New Edition (Thorley)
Which Oil? – Choosing the right oils & greases for your antique, vintage, veteran, classic or collector car (Michell)
Works MGs, The (Allison & Browning)
Works Minis, The Last (Purves & Brenchley)
Works Rally Mechanic (Moylan)

Discover more from Veloce's other imprints, featuring a wide range of general interest, animal care and children's books

www.veloce.co.uk

First published in September 2021 by Veloce Publishing Limited, Veloce House, Parkway Farm Business Park, Middle Farm Way, Poundbury, Dorchester DT1 3AR, England. Tel +44 (0)1305 260068 / Fax 01305 250479 / e-mail info@veloce.co.uk / web www.veloce.co.uk or www.velocebooks.com.
ISBN: 978-1-787111-85-1; UPC: 6-36847-01185-7.
© 2021 Anthony Bagnall and Veloce Publishing. All rights reserved. With the exception of quoting brief passages for the purpose of review, no part of this publication may be recorded, reproduced or transmitted by any means, including photocopying, without the written permission of Veloce Publishing Ltd. Throughout this book logos, model names and designations, etc, have been used for the purposes of identification, illustration and decoration. Such names are the property of the trademark holder as this is not an official publication. Readers with ideas for automotive books, or books on other transport or related hobby subjects, are invited to write to the editorial director of Veloce Publishing at the above address. British Library Cataloguing in Publication Data – A catalogue record for this book is available from the British Library. Typesetting, design and page make-up all by Veloce Publishing Ltd on Apple Mac. Printed in India by Replika Press.

Contents

ACKNOWLEDGEMENTS 5

FOREWORD 6

INTRODUCTION 7

CHAPTER ONE .... Pre-World War One (The Heroic Age) – 1900 to 1905 9

CHAPTER TWO .... The Heroic Age Continued – 1906 to 1914 19

CHAPTER THREE .... The Glorious 1920s 46

CHAPTER FOUR .... 1930s-1940s: A Quieter Period 65

CHAPTER FIVE .... The 1950s and a New Venture 85

CHAPTER SIX .... Fiat-based Specials 92

CHAPTER SEVEN .... Formula Junior 105

CHAPTER EIGHT .... Rallying: Fiat Returns 114

CHAPTER NINE .... The Abarth Connection 142

APPENDIX ONE .... Technical Details 150

APPENDIX TWO .... Competition Results 154

BIBLIOGRAPHY 156

INDEX 159

Acknowledgements

It is virtually impossible to acknowledge everybody who has contributed to this book, but I have received some marvellous assistance from certain individuals and organisations. There is no doubt in my mind that this book would not have been possible without the help I received from the staff at the *Centro Storico Fiat* (Fiat Museum) in Turin and Dr Marco Fazio, who is the Historical Services Manager for the entire Fiat Chrysler Automobile (FCA) group. In particular, their photographic archive for the period 1900 to 1927 was invaluable. You cannot imagine how pleased I was to discover that not only did the archive contain numerous photographs for this period but also comprehensive results listings for each year concerned. I doubt whether it would have been possible for me to have produced the details contained in Chapters 1, 2 and 3 without access to these records. Another invaluable source of information was the late Michael Sedgwick's book *Fiat*, published in 1974.

I am greatly indebted to Graham Robson for, in addition to agreeing to my using his book on the Fiat 131 Abarth for reference, letting me have free access to his photographic archive. Jon Day of the National Motor Museum at Beaulieu was also very helpful in granting me access to the museum's photographic archive. I must also say a very sincere 'thank you' to Duncan Rabagliatti, who is Chairman of the Historic Formula Junior Racing Association, for providing some period photographs of Formula Junior cars in action. He also generously offered, and undertook, the editing of Chapter 7 on Formula Junior. I must also mention my good friend Peter McFadyen who provided me with some of his excellent photographs, in particular those of the recreated 'Beast of Turin,' the Fiat S 76, at Chateau Impney. Thank you Peter!

There are also several photographs that I have used which are very old and in respect of which I have been unable to trace the original source, so if, as a consequence, I have inadvertently breached any copyrights, then I apologise most sincerely. Most of these photographs date from before the Second World War, making them at least 80 years old and it is likely that the original copyright holder is no longer alive. Also, I should add that a number of old photographs, particularly from the early 1900s, are not of very good quality and reproduction has suffered accordingly. This particularly applies to some of the early photographs obtained from the Fiat museum; they have been included due to their historic interest. Wherever possible, I have included drivers' full names, but in several instances this has not proved possible.

Finally, in terms of credits for photographs, I have used the following acronyms:
- FCA – Fiat Chrysler Automobiles, who are the owners of the *Centro Historico Fiat*
- NMM – the National Motor Museum at Beaulieu
- FF – Ferret Fotographics
- GR – Graham Robson
- DR – Duncan Rabagliatti
- PMcF – Peter McFadyen

Photographs with no credit attached have either been taken by myself at the Fiat Museum, the 2011 Mille Miglia and sundry motoring events, are in the public domain, or the originator cannot be identified. Since preparing this book, but before its publication, it was announced during January 2021 that a new company called 'Stellantis' had been formed with the merger of FCA and Groupe PSA. This new group now encompasses the former FCA brands and those of PSA, such as Peugeot, Citroën, Opel and Vauxhall. Due to the timing of this development, references to FCA remain unchanged in this book.

FOREWORD

When I decided to write the story of Fiat's involvement in motorsport, I certainly didn't appreciate the scope of this subject. I was very aware of Fiat's early endeavours in Grand Prix racing and of their successes in World Rally championships in the 1970s/early 1980s. However, I really didn't understand the extent to which the Fiat name has always been associated with motorsport, either directly or indirectly as an engine supplier. When, during the 1930s, '40s, '50s and '60s, they were not directly involved in terms of official works teams, etc. major events such as the Mille Miglia and Targa Florio usually had numerous Fiat entries, particularly in the smaller capacity classes. At national level, there were numerous events at which they featured, but there are too many to be included here, even if records do exist.

I was amazed at the number and variety of Fiats introduced during the early 1900s, especially the number of 'corsa' or racing models. The pace of development was outstanding. When one considers that the first corsa model, the 6 HP, in 1900 had a top speed of just 37mph and that by 1904, just four years later, the 75 HP was capable of nearly 100mph, the pace and scale of development can only be described as outstanding. Equally outstanding was the courage of those early racing drivers and their riding mechanics!

When investigating the Fiat specials, or 'etceterinis' as they are also called, there were so many that I cannot be sure that I have captured them all, so apologies for any that I have inadvertently omitted. The same comment can also be made in terms of the chapter on Fiat-powered Formula Junior cars. Further complications arise when considering the links between Simca and its designer, Amédée Gordini. Cisitalia and Abarth are other instances that complicate the story. In the case of Abarth, having been an independent manufacturer until 1971 when it was taken over by Fiat, it truly deserves a book of its own. I have mainly concentrated on the period under Fiat ownership when Abarth managed Fiat's racing department. A manufacturer that did present me with a problem was OSCA (I have used the normal spelling rather than the correct O.S.C.A. for simplicity), which produced cars with some Fiat components. However, apart from its Formula Junior car that was powered by a Fiat 1100 engine, its sports racing cars appeared to have only minimal Fiat components. Due to this, I have included OSCA in Chapter 6, but have not included it in the racing results, other than Formula Junior.

In the very earliest advertisements for Fiat cars the company name is correctly presented as 'F.I.A.T.' but appears to have been amended to the simpler 'Fiat' very quickly, which is what I have used throughout. Also early models tended to be described as '12 HP' for example, rather than simply '12hp' and so I have used the former style for consistency. In covering the early days of Fiat's involvement in Grand Prix and other racing events, I have relied on the information obtained from the Fiat archives in Turin. Where other accounts record a different result to that in the Fiat records, I have relied on the latter. Also, in converting distances, speeds, etc, from the metric measurement, I have used a factor of 1.609 kilometres to a mile which may result in some very minor discrepancies. As some of the results relate to events that happened over one hundred years ago, I am not sure that any such discrepancy is significant. Where race or lap times are quoted, I have just recorded hours and minutes, ignoring seconds in most cases as these times are just used to give an indication of the duration of events and not intended to be a wholly accurate record. Records in the *Centro Storico Fiat* list some events as 'Raids' – for example the records for 1908 list an event called *Raid Pietroburgo – Mosca*, I have assumed that this event was a road race/rally between St Petersburg and Moscow. There are other events described as 'Raids' and therefore I have assumed that these are races or rallies, usually over long distances. Also, I have included race times in places, this serves to indicate what a test of human endurance and courage was involved, particularly in the very early days.

Introduction

Today, many people think of Fiat as a manufacturer of small/medium-sized cars, with the occasional foray into sports cars such as the Fiat 124 Spider, which has now sadly ceased production. However, over its 120-year lifetime, Fiat has had many noteworthy competition successes, particularly in the very early days of Grand Prix racing, and, later, during the 1970s, international rallying. Fiat models, or Fiat-powered models, were also present in other forms of motorsport, and on several occasions even involved in World Land Speed Record attempts.

July 11, 1899 was a landmark date in the nascent Italian automobile industry. On that date the Fabbrica Italiana Automobili Torino (otherwise known as F.I.A.T.) was founded by a small group of Italian entrepreneurs, Cavaliere Giovanni Agnelli, Count Roberto Biscaretti di Ruffia, Count Emanuele Cacherano di Brichesario, and Cesare Goria-Gatti. Agnelli was a cavalry officer/amateur engineer, Biscaretti di Ruffia and Cacherano di Brichesario were aristocratic automobile enthusiasts, and Goria-Gatti a well known criminal lawyer. Agnelli, who was to become the dominant force within Fiat for many years, was not an aristocrat, but came from a family whose wealth came from the silk trade and agriculture. He had become a high-ranking cavalry officer, which assisted him in his business dealings due to the social importance given to such military figures in Italy in those days. The meeting held on that day was captured in a famous painting by Lorenzo Delleani, which today hangs in the *Centro Storico Fiat* (Fiat museum) in Turin.

Rather than starting from scratch, unlike many early automobile manufacturers, Fiat began by absorbing Ceirano Giovanni Battista & C, which produced bicycles and a light car. The light car involved had the curious English-sounding name of 'Welleyes' and consisted of a horizontal twin-cylinder, rear-mounted engine of 697cc (although some records suggest it was 663cc).

Delleani's painting of first shareholders' meeting.

The takeover provided the new company with a skilled labour force of about 50 workers and a business base in Turin. Included in the acquisition were the managing director, Enrico Marchesi, and the technical director, Aristide Faccioli. Also amongst the workforce inherited from Ceirano were two employees who were to feature prominently in Fiat's future sporting activities: Vincenzo Lancia and Felice Nazzaro.

The takeover of a going concern and the remarkable achievement of building and equipping a new factory in Turin allowed Fiat to produce its first car that year: the 3½ HP economy model, a modified version of the former 'Welleyes' model called the Tipo-A. There is a painting (artist unknown) hanging in the *Centro Historico*, which shows a family setting out on a journey in an early Fiat.

The first alteration to the Welleyes carried

out by Fiat was to replace the belt drive transmission by chain drive. By the first Turin Motor Show, held in May 1900, the engine capacity had been increased to 1082cc.

Meanwhile, Giovanni Ceirano, the eldest of the three brothers, left Fiat and started manufacturing cars under his own name. Together with his youngest brother, Matteo, he founded Fratelli Ceirano. The company survived the First World War, but had disappeared before the Second War. The Ceirano family certainly played a major role in the development of the Italian motor industry. Following the Fiat takeover of 1899, the middle brother of the Ceirano family, Giovanni, launched a new company, Società Ceirano Automobili Torino, under the acronym of 'Scat.' This survived until 1932 when it was taken over by Fiat. In 1903 Matteo Ceirano decided to establish his own company, and so Itala was born. Itala had a significant presence in competition, and achieved world-wide fame by winning the epic Peking to Paris race in 1907. The company lasted until 1934. However, in 1905 Matteo Ceirano left Itala to set up yet another company, this time with the name Società Piemontese Automobili, 'Spa.' This lasted until 1925 when it was absorbed into the growing Fiat empire. Thus it can be seen that the Ceirano brothers really did make a significant contribution to the early years of the Italian motor industry.

First Fiat model – 1899 3½ HP. (Courtesy FCA)

This painting of an early Fiat departure is displayed in Centro Historico.

CHAPTER ONE
Pre-World War One (The Heroic Age) – 1900 to 1905

It didn't take long for Fiat to start achieving success in competition, albeit in national events in Italy. It would be 1903 before Fiat was seen participating in international events. Although 1899 was Fiat's first year, a Fiat 'Welleyes' model took part in the Limone-Cuneo-Turin road race, and Cesare Goria-Gatti finished second in the 400kg category. Then, in the Padua-Bassano-Vicenza-Padua race, came Fiat's first racing victory; Vincenzo Lancia came first and Felice Nazzaro third. Another victory was achieved in the Turin to Asti road race when Castore was the outright winner and Biscaretti came first in the 'tourist' category. In April 1900, Castore, driving a 6 HP Corsa model, achieved Fiat's first outright victory in the Turin to Asti race, with Biscaretti winning the tourist class.

The 6 HP Corsa was designed by Faccioli, and was Fiat's first true competition model. It was a development of the Welleyes model, with the engine increased in size to 1082cc and the original belt drive transmission uprated to chain drive. It is, somewhat confusingly, referred to as the 6/8 HP model, as indeed it is in Fiat's own competition records.

Ing Giovanni Enrico on 1901 Fiat 8/12 HP. (Courtesy FCA)

A 46-mile race took place during May that ran from Bologna to Corticella, Poggio Renatico, Malalbergo and then back to Bologna. This time it was Agnelli driving one of his own creations, and he finished in second place in Category 4. Then, during July, a 130-mile race from Vincenza to Padua, via Bassano and Treviso, saw Lancia and Nazzaro finish first and second in their 6/8 HP Fiats. Lancia averaged 29.8mph for the race (this is according to Fiat's records, elsewhere it is claimed that both were disqualified for receiving outside assistance). In the same month, Lancia set a six mile record at 35.8mph, again driving a 6/8 HP model. September's results revealed more successes, with Lancia achieving second fastest at a three-mile record attempt at Brescia with a speed of 35mph. The same month saw Lancia again achieve second place, but this time in a 136-mile race from Brescia through Cremona, Mantua, Verona and back to Brescia. On December 9, Lancia took a class win in a 23-mile race from Turin to Chieri.

Change in design philosophy came about in 1901 when Faccioli left (or was he sacked?) due to disagreements with Agnelli over design issues. Faccioli stubbornly refused to consider any other configuration than rear-mounted twin-cylinder engines, whereas Agnelli saw the future as lying in front-mounted four-cylinder engines. Giovanni Enrico replaced Faccioli and immediately set about preparing front-engined four-cylinder models in line with Agnelli's wishes. Thus, 1901 saw the introduction of a new four-cylinder 12 HP model, which had a 3770cc engine. There was also a 'Corsa' racing version.

One of these new models, plus eight 8 HP 1082cc models, took part in the first automobile tour of Italy, the Giro d'Italia, which took place between April 27 and May 11, 1901. Sponsored by the newspaper *Il Corriere Della Sera*, the tour started in Turin and ended in Milan, the route having covered some 1000 miles. Included in the Fiat team was the organiser, Count Biscaretti of Ruffia. All 72 participants received a silver plate in recognition of their efforts and, despite many retirements amongst the other participants, the whole Fiat team completed the course.

Vincenzo Lancia

Vincenzo Lancia was born on August 24, 1881 in the village of Fobello in the Piedmont region of Italy, some 60 miles north east of Turin. He was the youngest of four children and his father was a wealthy businessman who had developed a successful business in Argentina before returning to Italy. Young Vincenzo demonstrated numeracy skills at an early age, but also developed a fascination for the motor car. He initially joined Ceirano in Turin where he had attended technical college. Interestingly, Ceirano's workshop was situated in the yard of the Lancia family's winter home in Turin. In a Ceirano official brochure published in 1899, Lancia is listed as 'contabile' or book-keeper/accountant. However, he was developing into a talented mechanic with a growing reputation amongst local car owners.

Lancia and Cierano's designer, Aristide Faccioli, became close friends, so when the newly formed Fiat company took over most of Ceirano's assets including Faccioli, Lancia was employed as Chief Inspector, although only 19 years of age. Recognising Lancia's skill as a driver, Fiat invited him to be a works driver alongside Felice Nazzaro. Thus his seven year career as a racing driver started. Lancia's exploits as a Fiat works driver are covered in some detail in Chapters 1 and 2 in this book. During November 1906, Lancia and Claudio Fogolin, a close friend and Fiat test driver, established a new company, Lancia & C Fabbrica Automobili. While developing his own cars, Fiat continued to employ him as a works driver, paying him handsomely. 1908 was his final season as a racing driver, with both Fiat and his own cars; his very last appearance as a driver was at the 1910 Modena Speed Trials where he recorded a class win in a 20hp Lancia Gamma.

Lancia's attention then was exclusively centred on developing Lancia cars, which he did very successfully until his early death in 1937 at the age of 56. Following his father's death, Gianni Lancia managed the company until 1956, when, on the verge of bankruptcy, the company was sold to Carlo Presenti, who sadly never managed to return Lancia to profitability. As a result, in 1969 Fiat took Lancia under its wing with the prime objective of keeping it Italian, as it had with Ferrari earlier.

1901 Fiat 12 HP Corsa. (Courtesy FCA)

Giovanni Agnelli and Felice Nazzaro on a Fiat 8 HP in the 1901 Giro d'Italia. (Courtesy FCA)

1902 Fiat 24 HP Corsa. (Courtesy FCA)

At Padua in a six mile event, Lazara, driving a 12 HP model, finished first in his category. There was a 50-mile contest between Piombino and Grosseto, which is on the west coast of Italy, south of Livorno and almost opposite the island of Elba. This event was won by Nazzaro, at the wheel of a 12 HP model. At 'Circuito di Livorno,' Nazzaro was again the winner in his 12 HP. Shortly afterwards the six mile Saluzzo trials were held, with Luigi Storero finishing first on two occasions. The year ended with two events close to Turin, including a hillclimb, and according to Fiat's own records, first places were achieved in both events, but the driver(s) are not recorded.

As in the previous years, Fiat's participation in 1902 was confined to events in Italy; it was another year before it was seen in international events outside its home country. There was a significant change to the cars that became a standard feature from then onwards: the adoption of a honeycomb radiator that was now considered to be the most efficient cooling system.

The first event, held at the beginning of

Storero's Fiat before the 1904 Gordon Bennett Cup. (Courtesy FCA)

Cagno in his 1904 Gordon Bennett car. (Courtesy NMM)

Felice Nazzaro at the 1904 Susa-Moncenisio hillclimb in his 75 HP Corsa. (Courtesy FCA)

June, was the 1300-mile Giro d'Italia in which Giovanni Agnelli, driving an 8 HP, was victorious. At the end of June, a 2.8-mile hillclimb was held at the nearby village of Sassi leading up to Superga. Driving a 24 HP Corsa model, Lancia set fastest time, whilst in a separate class Storero also set fastest time in a 12 HP model.

The 24 HP Corsa had a 6371cc four-cylinder engine and was the first Fiat to have an all-steel chassis. It was reputably capable of achieving a top speed of 60mph, which may not seem particularly fast today, but in 1902 must have seemed exceptional. On July 27, Lancia and Storero repeated their earlier successes in the 14-mile Susa to Moncenisio hillclimb.

The next Fiat successes came on October 14, when Storero and Lancia finished first and second respectively in their classes in a six-mile sprint at Padua. Additionally, Lancia and Storero finished second and third in a 0.6-mile record run driving their 24 HP and 12 HP models. The following day at Conegliano, which is a short distance north of Padua, once again Lancia and Storero finished first and second in a short sprint. During November there was a Fiat-Panhard match race at the Villanova-Bologna circuit that was won by a Fiat 12 HP Corsa model; similarly Nazzaro won a 187-mile challenge race between Turin and Bologna.

Although Fiat's participation in the international motor racing scene didn't officially start until the following year, during October in Portugal a 24 HP Fiat finished first, driven by the Duke of Porto and future star Pietro Bordino. The event from Figueras to Lisbon, is reported to have been Portugal's first ever motor race.

Vincenzo Lancia in a 75 HP Corsa winning the Brescia-Cremona-Mantua-Brescia race in 1904.

Lancia at the start of the 1905 Gordon Bennett Cup. (Courtesy NMM)

On May 24, 1903, two Fiats took part in the Light Car class of the ill-fated Paris to Madrid race. As is fairly well known, due to numerous crashes caused by dusty conditions and a lack of crowd control, five drivers and some spectators were killed; the race was cancelled at Bordeaux and the surviving cars taken back to Paris by horse and cart. This was the last of the epic city-to-city races. One Fiat had already retired, but Storero in his 24 HP model was in 17th place in his class when the race was stopped.

Following the accepted principle at the time that performance was directly related to engine capacity, in 1903 Fiat engineers built a four-cylinder engine with a capacity of no less than 10,603cc, giving the car a top speed in excess of 74mph. The engine consisted of two pairs of cylinders arranged in line, each cylinder having a capacity of 2650cc! The model was known as the 60 HP Corsa. This was in response to the Mercedes 60 that had a 9293cc engine. Most of these models went to the USA, and in events held in Readville and Boston during May and June, Hollander and Fogolin were victorious in their 60 HP models.

Back in Italy, June 12 saw the second running of the 12-mile Consuma Cup (Coppa Della Consuma) race and Storero and Lancia finished second and third respectively in the heavy car class, with Nazzaro winning in a Panhard. However, a Fiat took first place in the tourist class. On June 23, the light car class of the Circuit des Ardennes took place (the heavy car class had started the day before) and Alessandro Cagno driving a 24 HP model finished third, behind two 40hp cars, a Darracq and a Gobron-Brillié. Cagno's time for the six-lap, 318-mile race was 7h 6min, resulting in an average speed of 44.7mph. On October 25, Borsetto finished first in the light car class at a sprint near Padua. The final success of the year came in the Southport Speed Trials during October, when Miller was victorious in a 24 HP Fiat.

For 1904, modifications to the 24 HP model included an increase in capacity to 6902cc. On May 20, a 500-mile contest for touring cars was held. Starting from Milan it was won by a Fiat driven by Schott, taking 20h 40min to complete the course, representing an average speed of 24mph. The first major international event of 1904 was the Gordon Bennett Cup on June 17. As the 1903 event had been won by Camille Jenatzy driving a Mercedes, under the rules it was Germany's turn to organise that year's event. For this important 318-mile race, Fiat entered a team of three 14,112cc 'monsters,' rated at 76hp, and to be driven by Lancia, Cagno and Storero. Once again the engine configuration was of four cylinders in two pairs mounted in-line formation. Designated the '75 HP Corsa,' these huge-engined cars could achieve a maximum speed of approximately 100mph! Under the rules for the Gordon Bennett Cup series cars had to be painted in a colour that represented their country, at that time Italy had been allocated black as its national colour (changed to red some time later), emphasising the already awesome appearance of these giant racing cars. However, this was not to be Fiat's day, as the highest-placed Fiat was driven by Lancia into eighth place, Cagno was tenth, and Storero retired after completing only two of the four laps.

In the 14-mile Susa-Moncenisio hillclimb, Lancia was once again fastest in his 75 HP model, with Cagno third and Storero fifth.

The next significant win for Fiat came at the end of September in the 231-mile Brescia-Cremona-Mantua-Brescia road race, also known as the 'Florio Cup,' when Lancia was the outright winner. Driving a 75 HP model, he took 3h 12min to complete the course, resulting in an average speed of 72mph. Team-mate Cagno finished in sixth place. Shortly afterwards, the Consuma Cup meeting saw victories in classes for Lancia (75 HP) and Cagno (60 HP). In the touring class Cagno was followed by two more Fiats in second and third position.

Moving away from Europe, in India, Gropelli, driving a 16 HP model, won the touring class in the Delhi-Bombay trials. The 16 HP model could be purchased in either landaulet (saloon) or phaeton (open) versions, powered by a four-cylinder engine with a capacity of 4179cc, which from 1906 was increased to 4503cc.

In the USA, whilst both the Fiats entered in the Vanderbilt Cup were eliminated, there were several successes elsewhere. At the Empire City track near New York, a team of three 75 HP Fiats, led by William Wallace, finished first, second and third in their class. Ormond Beach in Florida saw a Fiat set a record time for a mile travelling at approximately 100mph. An 80-mile handicap race at Daytona resulted in a Fiat victory, and finally, at the Eagle Rock hillclimb, records show that, led by Wallace, Fiat scored a one-two-three victory in a class for cars costing more than $5000. However, in a class for cars weighing up to 2240lb they were beaten by a Renault driven by Maurice Bernin.

For the 1905 racing season, Fiat produced an even larger car, the 100 HP Corsa, which was powered by a 16,286cc four-cylinder overhead valve engine. This 100hp car was capable of over 100mph and had the largest engine built by Fiat up to that date. The first success of the year came in January at Daytona Beach in the USA, when Paul Sartori finished first in the 50-mile handicap race driving his 90 HP model. (Author's note: I have been unable to find any details of this model and I am wondering whether it was an uprated 75 HP?) July 1905 saw the final Gordon Bennett Cup race take place in France; this was due primarily to the French objecting to only being allowed to enter three

Poster showing 1904/1905 Gordon Bennett teams. (Courtesy NMM)

Lancia practising for the 1905 Gordon Bennett Cup in the 110 HP. (Courtesy NMM)

Nazzaro at the 1905 Gordon Bennett Cup. (Courtesy FCA)

cars when there were many makes that could compete. Another factor in its demise was the fact that apparently James Gordon Bennett now considered the event to be too commercialised, and he turned his attention to ballooning and then aircraft. Due to the fact that Leon Théry had won the previous year's race driving a French car, a Richard-Brasier, under the rules it was France's turn to organise the 1905 and final Gordon Bennett Cup. The race was held over five laps of an 85-mile course in the Auvergne, and Fiat entered three cars to be driven by Lancia, Nazzaro and Cagno. The course, which had to be lapped four times, was described in one contemporary journal in the following terms: "To describe in detail would be something like detailing a 'looping the loop' performance. It is all twisting and turning, climbing up and down." The longest straight was only about 2½ miles long, so it was clearly very demanding of both driver and car. The cars entered were the 16,286cc-engined models, but tuned to run at 1200rpm compared with the 1100rpm of the usual 100 HP models, giving them an additional 10bhp, thus justifying the title of the '110 HP Gordon Bennett Corsa.' In the early stages of the race Lancia was in first place with a substantial lead when disaster struck and he was forced to retire at the end of the third lap with a seized engine as a result of a leaking radiator. However, it was not all bad news for Fiat as Nazzaro and Cagno finished second and third, respectively, and Lancia had set the fastest lap before retiring; his time represented a fastest lap of just under 57mph. On July 16, Fiat repeated its earlier successes in the 14-mile Susa to Moncenisio hillclimb when Nazzaro and Cagno finished first and second in their class; they were both driving 100 HP models. At some point in 1905, Fiat produced the poster/advertisement identifying the two teams that had taken part in both the 1904 and 1905 Gordon Bennett races, although they have mixed up the years, as Storero was in the 1904 team and Nazzaro in the 1905 team.

In the USA on August 28, Emanuele Cedrino was victorious in a match race between Los Angeles and New York; he was driving a 24 HP model. Three weeks later Fiat entered Lancia and Cagno in the Mont Ventoux hillclimb in France. Unfortunately, Lancia had engine problems, but Cagno upheld Fiat's honour by finishing first and setting a new record of 19min 18.5s in his 100 HP model. The second Vanderbilt Cup was held in the USA on October 15. Fiat entered three 100 HP cars to

Cagno was fastest at Mont Ventoux in his 100 HP. (Courtesy FCA)

Lancia on a 60 HP Corsa at the start of an unidentifiable event. (Courtesy FCA)

be driven by Lancia, Nazzaro and Swiss driver Louis Chevrolet, who was later to become a well known motor manufacturer in his own right. Lancia stormed into a lead that he held for seven laps, but then on lap eight, because he was more than a complete lap ahead, he decided to have a precautionary pit stop to change tyres, resulting in his clashing with another competitor's car. The time taken to effect repairs meant that he lost the lead and eventually finished a furious fourth, having the only compensation of setting the fastest lap in 23min 18s.

Fiat's USA season did produce some compensation after the disaster of the Vanderbilt Cup. Lancia and Cedrino scored victories in Florida and Providence respectively; further successes came at Poughkeepsie, New York, Empire City, Hartford, Morris Park and Cape May. Finally, back in Italy, a reliability trial in Milan saw Fiat cars finish in first place in three classes.

The evocative photograph above of the start of a race is from the Fiat archive, and is described as 'Lancia sur Fiat da corse'. The photograph is dated 1905, but the event is not identified. The car appears to be a 60 HP Corsa, but it has not proved possible to discover the actual event. It may have been in the USA where Fiat was very active.

Chapter Two
The Heroic Age Continued – 1906 to 1914

The first success for Fiat in 1906 came early. On January 15-16, in the 310-mile Swedish Winter Cup rally between Gothenburg and Stockholm, a 24 HP Fiat driven by Emil Salmson came first, taking 26h 45min to complete the event. This was his first in a series of wins in this event; photographs show that he was accompanied by three passengers, all of them, including Salmson, dressed in heavy fur coats, which must have been essential wear in a Scandinavian winter event. In the same month the Daytona Speed Trials took place and proved to be a Darracq benefit, although Fiat scored several class wins in the hands of Lancia and Cedrino.

The first ever motor race in Cuba took place on February 12, and Fiat entered two cars to be driven by Lancia and Cedrino. The race was based in Havana and was 217 miles long; President Palma attended, accompanied by his army guards. Unfortunately it wasn't Fiat's lucky day; Lancia went out on the first lap, after his mechanic fell out of the car and broke a leg, and Cedrino later crashed, which also eliminated him.

May 6 1906 saw the first Targa Florio take place in Sicily, initiated by wealthy Sicilian, Vincenzo Florio. This touch race around the island existed until 1973, but then the CSI announced that the race would no longer be a round of the World Sports Car Championship and so it never took place again. The first event was for standard cars, with certain price and weight conditions. Only ten cars started, one of which was a Fiat 28/40 HP driven by Lancia, who unfortunately retired with mechanical problems on the last lap. The 28/40 HP had a 7363cc four-cylinder engine and subsequently became known as the '28/40 HP Targa Florio Corsa.' Lancia had been in second place on lap one, but a leaking fuel tank dropped him to seventh before he eventually retired with a cracked cylinder.

As a number of European countries, including Britain and Germany, were holding long distance touring car events, the Italian newspaper, *Corriere della Sera*, organised a 2485-mile touring car event called the Coppa d'Oro to be held on May 15. This started from Milan and finished two weeks later back in Milan, having been through Verona, Padua, Bologna, Rome, Naples, Florence, Genoa and Turin en route. Against a comprehensive list of starters, Lancia finished first with no penalties, and team mates Nazzaro and Boschis were fourth and fifth respectively, thereby winning the team prize for Fiat. Lancia was driving a 24/40 HP.

During June, the Herkomer Trophy rally took place in Southern Germany and Emil Mathis won a Gold Medal. There is some confusion as to which model Fiat he was driving, as it was reported as a 28/40 HP, a sports/racer, although the event was supposed to be for touring cars. The event, organised by Anglo/German artist Hubert Herkomer, only took place on three occasions, 1905 to 1907.

With the cessation of the Gordon Bennett Cup series of races, the Automobile Club de France (ACF) organised the first French Grand Prix to be held on a 64-mile triangular course near Le Mans on June 26-27. Two bypass roads were constructed specially for the event, enabling certain towns to be bypassed and

Mathis collected a gold medal at the 1906 Herkomer Trial. (Courtesy FCA)

Nazzaro at scrutineering for 1906 French GP.

avoiding having to race down very narrow streets. Unfortunately these bypass roads were constructed from wood, and became very dangerous as the race progressed. The lack of restriction on the number of cars from each participating country, as was the case with the previous Gordon Bennett Cup races, resulted in a large number of entries. Fiat entered three cars to be driven by Lancia, Nazzaro and Dr Aldo Weillschott, who was a director of Fiat's New York agency, Hollander and Tangerman. The cars were the 1905 100 HP models that had the massive four-cylinder 16,286cc overhead valve engine. At the start, both Nazzaro and Weillschott stalled, so by the end of the first lap Nazzaro was only in 14th place, but, remarkably, the amateur Weillschott was in fourth place, actually ahead of team-mate Lancia in fifth place! It was a two day race and at the end of day one Weillschott had retired having reached third place on the second lap, Lancia had slipped back to ninth place, and Nazzaro had recovered from his poor start to reach third place behind leader Ferenc Szisz with his Renault and Albert Clément in his Clément-Bayard. After a long race run in very hot conditions, bad road surfaces and numerous tyre changes, Szisz came home first, but Nazzaro managed to beat Clément into second place. Nazzaro had taken 12h 14min to complete the race over the two days, and had averaged 60.4mph. Lancia eventually managed to regain his first lap position of fifth. This race had clearly demonstrated the advantages of having detachable rims to aid tyre changes, as fitted to the winning Renault and the Fiats.

The next important international event was the Vanderbilt Cup Race which took place on October 6 on Long Island, New York. The race was over ten laps of the 20-mile course giving a race distance of 297.1 miles. Louis Wagner, driving a Darracq, took an immediate lead which he

Nazzaro's mechanic starts his car at the start of the 1906 French GP. (Courtesy NMM)

The Heroic Age Continued – 1906 to 1914

1906 French GP – Nazzaro cornering.

The first major race of the season was the Targa Florio held on April 21 over the mountainous Madonie circuit. The previous year's regulations were scrapped and, for this race, entries were to be limited to cars with four-cylinder engines which had to have cylinder bores of between 120mm and 130mm. A minimum weight requirement of 1000kg was introduced, with an extra 20kg added for each millimetre of cylinder bore over the 120mm figure. The circuit and duration was the same as previously, ie three laps of the 92.27-mile circuit. The race attracted 19 different makes and 46 entries. Fiat entered three 28/40 HP cars for Lancia, Nazzaro and Weillschott. At the end of the first lap, Lancia was in first place with Nazzaro in fourth place. The other Fiat entry, Weillschott, was in twelfth place. Nazzaro took the lead on the next lap and held it to the end of the race; meanwhile, Lancia, having slipped back to third place on the second lap, eventually finished second. Weillschott climbed through the field to finish in eighth place. The team had been allocated the number 20 for the race, with Nazzaro's car carrying the number 20B. He covered the 277 miles in 8h 17min 36s, representing an average speed of 33.5mph. Lancia set the fastest lap at 34mph. Nazzaro's car, or possibly a recreation, has been displayed over the years, and in 2011 could be seen at NEC's (National Exhibition Centre) classic car show.

held until the end of the race. Driving his 130 HP Fiat, Lancia finished second, some three minutes later, having narrowly beaten Arthur Duray in a De Dietrich. Lancia's time for the race was 4h 53min, equating to an average speed of 60.3mph. Nazzaro retired on the 10th and final lap, but still placed sixth, while Weillschott failed to complete a single lap.

The 130 HP was a development of the 16,286cc 110 HP model; once again the increase in power came about via further tuning that increased the maximum rpm to 1600, as distinct from the 1200rpm of the earlier model. According to records kept at Fiat Museum, Fiats scored a one-two-three at a five-mile event held at the Empire City Track; other than the year 1906, the records do not give the precise date of the event nor which models were used.

After a somewhat lacklustre year for Fiat, 1907 proved to be all that they wished for, indeed it has been described as their 'Annus Mirabilis.' However, the year also experienced a severe economic recession, caused by the so-called 'Agadir Crisis' that triggered diplomatic tensions between Germany and Britain and its allies. Firms went bankrupt overnight with the automobile sector hard hit. Luckily, or perhaps due to foresight, Fiat survived relatively unscathed because of its diversity in producing many non-automobile items. An unusual feature of this season was that the three major events were held under differing formulae.

The first recorded successes came in February when both Lancia and Cedrino recorded wins at an event in Florida. During the same month, Salmson scored his second successive win in the Swedish Winter Cup rally in his 24 HP Fiat.

Nazzaro – winner of the 1907 Targa Florio. (Courtesy FCA)

Lancia prepares for the start of the 1907 Targa Florio. (Courtesy FCA)

June saw the inaugural Kaiserpreis race take place in Germany, run as a race for touring cars with a maximum engine size of eight litres. The circuit chosen passed through Homburg, Oberursel, Königstein, Esch, Weilmunster, Weilburg, Usingen, and Wehrheim, and included sections of the earlier Gordon Bennett course. Fiat had again entered three cars, this time for Lancia and Nazzaro as usual, but with Wagner in the third car. For this event, Fiat had gone to the trouble (and expense!) of building three special cars that became known as the 'Taunus Corsa' models. They were fitted with 8004cc four-cylinder overhead valve engines with a power output of 72bhp and a top speed of 81mph. There were 92 entries for the race, which meant that the organisers had no option other than to hold two eliminating races

The Heroic Age Continued – 1906 to 1914

'20B' at the 2011 NEC classic car show.

in order to reduce the number of starters to 40; this was considered to be the maximum number that could be safely accommodated. Lancia competed in the first eliminating race, which he duly won, and Nazzaro and Wagner ran in the second, finishing first and second respectively. In the race itself, Nazzaro, driving car number 8B, eventually won, having at one stage dropped to third behind Lucien Hautvast and Charles Deplus in their Pipes. Wagner eventually finished fifth, closely followed by Lancia. Nazzaro's time for the 293-mile race was 5h 34min 26s, an average speed of 52.5mph. Nazzaro was presented with his prize from the German Emperor, Kaiser Wilhelm II. Only one Kaiserpreis race took place, as the following year it was replaced by the Prinz-Heinrich-Fahrt which took place from 1908 until 1911. It was named after the Kaiser's brother, who was a motoring enthusiast. Interestingly, the winner in 1910 was none other than Ferdinand Porsche who later became famous for the manufacture of cars under his own name.

Less than three weeks later, on July 2, the second French Grand Prix took place. Unlike the first race, the circuit chosen was based on Dieppe, the lap was shorter at 47 miles and the race restricted to one day only. This was in acknowledgement that the previous year's race had put too much physical strain on both the drivers and their mechanics. It was a triangular circuit similar to the previous year at Le Mans, but shorter and better surfaced, with no wooden sections. The formula chosen did not limit engine size, but stipulated a maximum petrol consumption of 9.41mpg (30 litres per 100km). Fiat entered three 16,286cc 130 HP cars tuned to meet the new fuel consumption formula. The drivers were the same trio as at the Kaiserpreis, numbered F1 – Lancia, F2 – Nazzaro and F3 – Wagner. The first three laps of the ten lap race saw Wagner leading Duray in his Lorraine-Dietrich, then Wagner retired leaving Lancia to battle with Duray. In lap nine Duray retired with a seized gearbox and shortly afterwards, on the tenth and final lap, Lancia had clutch trouble and also retired. However, once again it was Nazzaro's day; he won at an average speed of 70.5mph, beating Szisz's Renault by just over six minutes. His time for the ten lap, 477-mile race was 6h 46min. Nazzaro was presented with his prize by a Cabinet Minister, Mr Barthou, with the following address "A year ago, when you placed yourself second in this same competition, I had congratulated you on your achievement; this year, I am delighted to see that you placed yourself first; this you have well deserved."

1907 was clearly Fiat and Nazzaro's year, having won the three major races that year. It has been recorded that during the late summer, Giovanni Agnelli met with friends at a coffee shop in Turin and placed three cards on the table. Each card bore a number, 20B, 8B and F2, which of course represented the numbers of the three victorious cars. He allegedly said that the cards "represented victories in the three most important races of the year, which established our (Fiat's) supremacy without question." Fiat also took the opportunity to maximise the publicity benefit of these results, as can be seen from the poster displayed at the 1907 Olympia Motor Show in London (see page 26).

Apart from the aforementioned races, other lesser events took place with Fiat's involvement. There was a marathon event from St Petersburg to Moscow that saw a class win for Fokin driving a Fiat 'Brevetti.' The 'Brevetti' was a 15/20 HP touring car with a 3052cc engine; it was a product of the Fiat takeover of Ansaldo. A first place was also achieved in a Concours d'Elegance event at Bombay by a local agent's entry of a 24/40 HP limousine. In the USA some successes were achieved at Morris Park and New York. The first races at the Brooklands circuit in England took place on July 6, but it proved not to be a successful outing for Wagner as he unsuccessfully took part in both the Marcel Renault and Byfleet Memorial Plates. However, Kishichiro Okura finished second in the Montagu Cup in his 120 HP Fiat. Okura was a Japanese baron who was responsible for introducing the motor car to Japan.

1908 started on a high for Fiat. Salmson scored his third successive win in the Swedish Winter Cup rally, once again driving his trusty 24 HP model. Then in March, Cedrino, driving

Lancia's car being fuelled before the start of the 1907 French Grand Prix.

Felice Nazzaro

Born in Turin on December 14, 1881, the son of a local coal merchant, Felice Nazzaro started work as a teenager in the Ceriano workshops, eventually becoming a mechanic. In a similar situation to Lancia, when Fiat took over Ceirano they inherited the young Nazzaro. Somewhat quieter than his ebullient team-mate, Lancia, he would hang back initially, biding his time before surging through to win after many of his competitors had failed. His first victory came in 1901, and by 1905 he was an official member of the Fiat racing team alongside Lancia. His greatest year was 1907 when he won the three major races held. He continued to score victories for Fiat, but the firm's racing activities were gradually being curtailed, and so, like Lancia, he founded his own company 'Nazzaro & C Fabbrica di Automobili' in Turin. He did score some race wins in his own cars, but the company did not prosper and ceased to exist after 1923.

After the First World War, Fiat returned to racing and Nazzaro rejoined the team, scoring several important victories. Sadly, in 1923 his wife died in a car accident, and as a consequence he retired from active racing. Fiat continued to employ him as head of competitions until it finally withdrew from racing in 1929. Felice Nazzaro, who was always gentlemanly in both his driving and behaviour, and immaculate in dress, died in Turin on March 21, 1940 at the age of 59 years, after a long illness.

the Fiat 'Cyclone,' scored three wins at the Ormonde-Daytona speed event, including a 186-mile race for the America Cup in which he averaged just over 77mph. A degree of mystery surrounds the Cyclone, some are of the opinion that it had been a Kaiserpreis car, whilst an alternative view is that it was derived from a Gordon Bennett model; it now seems unlikely that, due to the passage of time, this matter will never be satisfactorily resolved.

On April 24, the Briarcliff Trophy race took place in Winchester County, New York; this event only took place once. Fiat entered two cars to be driven by Cedrino and Ed Parker. Cedrino, driving the 'Cyclone,' finished second to Lewis Strang's Isotta-Fraschini; sadly, this was to be Cedrino's last race as a month later

The Heroic Age Continued – 1906 to 1914

Roadside repairs by Lancia and his mechanic at the 1907 French Grand Prix.

he died in a practice crash at Baltimore. An interesting incident took place at one of the American tracks when an 18-year-old college boy managed to persuade Cedrino to let him have a drive in his Fiat; this was David Bruce-Brown, who was soon to feature prominently in Fiat's racing activities.

The first major European race of 1908 was the Targa Florio on May 18. Unlike the previous year when 46 drivers of 19 different manufacturers participated, only 16 drivers of seven different manufacturers were entered, and only 13 actually started. Fiat entered Lancia and Nazzaro driving the 28/40 HP models, and the former led the race until delayed with tyre problems. It had been a very close race with only 19 seconds covering the first four at the end of the first lap. Lancia still managed to finish second, albeit some 13 minutes behind the winner, Vincenzo Trucco in his Isotta-

Lancia's car retiring from the 1907 French Grand Prix.

FIAT IN MOTORSPORT SINCE 1899

Nazzaro's French GP winner in the Centro Historico. (Courtesy FCA)

Fraschini. Nazzaro had steering failure and consequently only managed to complete two laps of the three-lap race, nevertheless he was still credited with eighth place, and before his technical problems he managed to set the fastest lap of the day at 36.17mph.

The following day, many hundreds of miles away in Russia, the 438-mile race from St Petersburg to Moscow took place. Fiat had several entries, but no doubt due to the proximity to the Targa Florio, these did not include Lancia and Nazzaro. The entries in Class I included Vincenzo Florio and Bosardé, Class II Wagner, and in Class III the Russian driver, Alexander Fokin. Neither Florio nor Bosardé finished, but Wagner, driving an 18/24 HP touring model, came first in his class and was

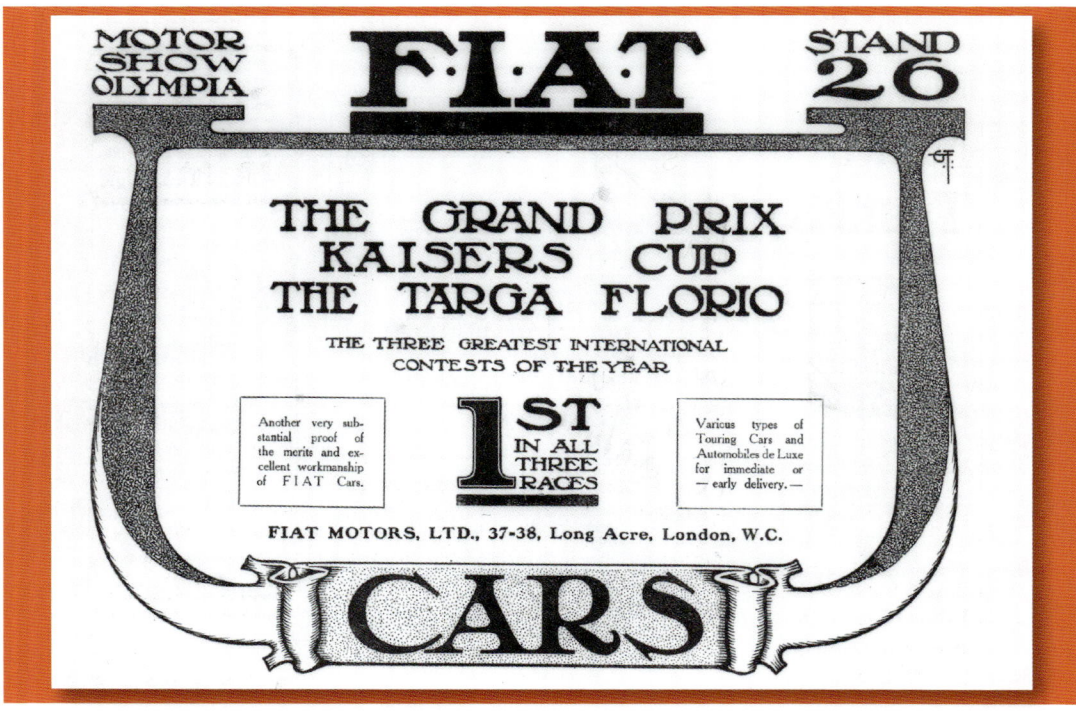

1907 Olympia Motor Show poster. (Courtesy FCA)

26

Lancia in number 1A lines up for the start of the 1908 Targa Florio. (Courtesy NMM)

third overall; Fokin, driving a 'Brevetti' model, once again won his class, finishing fourth overall. Still in Russia, at a meeting in Moscow, a Fiat 60 HP is recorded as setting a speed record of 63mph, over what distance or the identity of the driver is not recorded.

On June 8, Brooklands witnessed an unusual international event. Selwyn Edge, who had a major interest in Napier cars and recognised the importance of motorsport as a promotional tool, challenged Fiat to a match race against a Napier on the Brooklands track. Fiat sent Nazzaro with a 175hp SB 4 Corsa model and Napier entered a six-cylinder 90hp model known as 'Samson.' The 175hp SB 4 model was fitted for this event with a four-cylinder engine of 18,146cc, a true monster! The Napier, driven by Frank Newton, broke its crankshaft and therefore Nazzaro was the winner. During the race Nazzaro was timed electrically at 121.64mph, although manually it was only timed at 107.98mph; this has been the subject of controversy ever since.

July 7 saw the third running of the Grand Prix in France. It was held on the same course as in 1907 and 46 entries were received, including three from Fiat to be driven by Lancia, Nazzaro and Wagner. The Fiats were the 12,045cc SB 4 models. Both Nazzaro and Wagner led at some point early in the race, but retired before half distance with engine problems. Lancia only managed to complete one lap before he too retired. At this stage it had become clear that Fiat wasn't going to repeat its glorious achievements of the previous year.

The next appearance of the Grand Prix Fiats was on September 6 at Bologna. This meeting comprised two races: the Coppa Florio for Grand Prix cars and the Targa Bologna for types of cars that had taken part in the Targa Florio.

*Lancia in the SB4 Corsa.
(Courtesy NMM)*

Fiat entered three 12,045cc SB 4 models in the Coppa Florio, to be driven by Lancia, Nazzaro and Wagner. Lancia in his 12-litre car took an immediate lead, which he kept until the fifth lap when mechanical troubles intervened, but he managed to complete the race, eventually finishing fifth. He did, however, have the consolation of setting the fastest lap at a speed of 82.3mph. This event was notable for Fiat in that it was Lancia's final drive in a works Fiat. Wagner's car suffered a broken axle and he retired on the fifth lap. All was not lost for Fiat however, as Nazzaro won at an average speed of 74.1mph for the ten-lap, 328-mile race, with a time of 4h 25min.

The European season had finished and the next race for Fiat was in the USA. On November 26 the Automobile Club of America held its 'Grand Prize' race in Savannah which attracted all the best European drivers, in stark contrast to the Vanderbilt Cup Race that, run under different rules, was an almost totally American affair. Wagner won the 402-mile race, with Nazzaro in third place, having led until he was delayed by a puncture. The third Fiat, driven by Ralph de Palma in his first race for the team, set fastest lap at 69.5mph and finished in ninth place after overcoming several problems that had dropped him down to 16th place. Wagner's time for the race was 6h 10min, resulting in an average speed of 65.2mph. An unusual statistic accompanying the results was speed over a flying mile: while Wagner achieved 90.0mph and team-mate Nazzaro 86.9mph, the fastest was Strang's Renault at an astonishing 101.7mph, followed by Hanriot's Benz at 100.0mph. The Fiats were the S61 Corsa models, which had a four-cylinder, 10,087cc, overhead valve engine that produced 115bhp and a maximum speed in excess of 93mph. These models competed in numerous events in the USA between 1908 and 1912.

Several less important event successes are recorded in the Fiat archives in Turin, these include a first place in the Coppa di Minneapolis in the USA, a first in Brazil, Argentina at the Mar del Plata, and in San Sebastian in Northern Spain; in none of these results is the driver or type of Fiat recorded. In Britain, James Radley, who was to become famous later as an aviator, made fastest time of the day at the Luton Hoo hillclimb in his 28/40 HP Fiat.

At the end of 1908, a consortium of leading manufacturers had decided not to continue in motorsport, so Grand Prix racing was in abeyance for three years. A conference, involving countries that organised international motor races, met during October and proposed holding the Grand Prix in 1909 on a circuit near Anjou, to be run under a

Lancia in the pits at the 1908 Florio Cup. (Courtesy NMM)

new formula for four-cylinder engines, with restrictions on bore size and minimum weight. However, by the end of December, only three teams had entered and consequently the race was cancelled. This situation had a major impact on European racing, with only the Targa Florio continuing through this period. However, in the USA, racing continued to be very popular and prospered. As a result two European manufacturers turned their attention to the USA in order to increase their visibility, and, hopefully, profits. The two were Fiat and Benz.

1909 saw another significant change at Fiat. Giovanni Enrico, who had replaced Aristide Faccioli as chief designer/engineer in 1901, died that year. He had supported Agnelli tirelessly over the years and had introduced many new designs. His replacement was Guido Fornaca, who was to remain with Fiat throughout the glorious Grand Prix era in charge of the Technical Department until his early death in 1928. During Fornaca's tenure he had undoubtedly played a major role in assuring Fiat's pre-eminence as a leading innovator in the automobile world. It is somewhat ironic that his death occurred shortly after Fiat had withdrawn from motor racing.

As already noted, the only important European race left on the 1909 calendar was the Targa Florio. This took place on May 2; however, it was a shadow of its former self, consisting of just one lap of the 92.27-mile Madonie circuit. In addition to the general malaise that European racing was experiencing, Sicily had suffered a major earthquake at Messina earlier in the year. This had caused a large number of fatalities, so it was surprising that the race took place at all, though no surprise that the entry was so small.

Nazzaro leaving the pits at the 1908 Florio Cup. (Courtesy NMM)

Wagner in number 14 before the start of the Grand Prize race at Savannah. (Courtesy FCA)

Just 11 cars started and no works Fiats were entered, although Florio had entered his own Fiat, a tourer stripped for racing. He finished second behind a SPA driven by Baron Francesco Ciuppa; Florio's average speed for the 92 miles was just under 34mph.

During the same month, the 'Riunione di Modena' speed trials were held, and a Fiat was successful in category VIII, the driver and model are not recorded in the Fiat archive. Outside Italy, a race was held between Moscow and Twer in Russia (Twer is a city north-west of Moscow that had its name changed to Kalinin in 1931). Fiats were successful in three classes, although the drivers are not recorded, the models involved are reported as a 15/20 HP and two 50/60 HPs. Both were touring cars, the 15/20 had a 2612cc engine, and the 50/60s a 9017cc engine, each engine being front-mounted with four cylinders and side-valves. At a hillclimb event near Marchiruz in Switzerland, Fiats had a very successful outing: in addition to an overall win there were also three class wins. Once again, unfortunately, the Fiat archive does not record details of the drivers or models of Fiat involved. At a sprint event titled the Coppa Mégevet, near Nancy in France, Fiats scored two first and second places in different classes. The winning driver was Emil Mathis, who was also victorious in a sprint meeting near Brussels. Fiats finished first in a hillclimb near Boulogne, first, second and third in a race meeting near Frankfurt, and a 12/15 HP finished first in the 560-mile Strasbourg to Semmering Raid. The 12/15 HP may have been the 3052cc Brevetti Type 2 – the Type 1 had been the first Fiat to have transmission via a propeller shaft, rather than the usual chain drive, or it may have been a 'Zero' model. Both of these models had an 1846cc side-valve engine.

The American season continued unabated and saw several Fiat victories. Wins were recorded in Grand Rapids, Atlanta, and Minneapolis, but as neither the drivers, nor the Fiat models involved, are named it can be assumed that they were local drivers and that the Fiats are likely to have been the 10,087cc S61 Corsa models that appeared in many events in the USA. However, at Riverhead it was de Palma in his Fiat who won. Another event where the driver is identified is in the Vanderbilt Cup race when Edward Parker drove his Fiat into second place; three cars had been entered for Parker, Lewis Strang and Eddie Hearne, but only Parker completed the race.

Fiat did not enter the 1910 Targa Florio, which had been increased to two laps; the

Wagner leads the Grand Prize at Savannah. (Courtesy FCA)

entry list was small and only two cars were classed as finishers. In this period it was Fiat alone which continued to produce special racing cars, all of which were based on its 1908 types. In particular the road-racing models were primarily designed for the Grand Prize and Indianapolis races in the USA, European hillclimbs and miscellaneous events. In a home event, the Riunione di Modena, Fiats driven by Bordino, Nazzaro and Boschis managed to win their classes. In the big-car class Nazzaro won at a speed of 84.6mph. The Bollinger Cup hillclimb was held in Switzerland and resulted in a win for Mathis. In Austria, Schudt was third in the big car class at Semmering. Other European victories took place in events held in Marseille, Valencia and San Sebastian. The win in Valencia also included winning the Royal Automobile Club of Spain's cup.

In South America, there were victories for Fiat in Mar del Plata, where Fiats finished in first place in five different categories, and also in Buenos Aires. In Russia two victories were recorded. One of the Russian victories was in a 230-mile Raid event from Moscow to Orel

In the USA, a 90hp (presumably an S61 model) set a series of distance records at events near Los Angeles, Atlanta, Narbeth and Syracuse.

Due to the fact that at the end of 1908, the manufacturers of racing cars had decided not to participate in Grands Prix, by 1911 motor racing in Europe was most definitely in the doldrums. Once again there were no official Fiat entries in the 1911 Targa Florio race, which had now been increased to three laps. Interestingly, during this period Lancia was now producing his own cars,

Nazzaro and Bordino in their S61 models. (Courtesy FCA)

and the 1911 race saw Cortese finish second in his Lancia, having set the fastest lap of the race. This situation continued until 1912 when Grand Prix racing proper resumed.

In France, despite several unsuccessful attempts by the ACF to organise a Grand Prix, it was a young club, the Automobile Club de L'Ouest, that organised the Grand Prix de France to be run on a circuit near Le Mans. This race had the full support of the ACF, but unfortunately attracted only 14 entries, of which only Fiat, with one car, and Rollard-Pilain, with three cars, were works entries. Despite the absence of other major manufacturers, Fiat had clearly thought that it was worth participating, and on July 23 1911, Victor Hémery took his S61 to victory. The race was run under Formula Libre rules, and Hémery's average speed for the 12-lap, 403-mile race was 55.71mph. He also set the fastest lap at a speed of 68.00mph and took 7h 6min to complete the race. The paucity of strong competitors can be seen by the fact that second place was taken by a 1300cc Bugatti driven by Ernest Friderich, who was two laps down, followed by the highest placed Rolland-Pilain driven by Fernand Gabriel. During the race Hémery did not have it all his own way as Maurice Fournier, the younger brother of the well known driver Henri Fournier, was challenging the Fiat for the lead in his Corre La Licorne when Fournier crashed on the sixth lap resulting in his death, in addition to that of his onboard mechanic.

Presumably, in part due to the state of road racing in Europe and the importance of its US customer base, Fiat's attention switched to the other side of the Atlantic Ocean. Bearing in mind the fact that a manufacturing plant had been opened during 1908 in Poughkeepsie located in New York State, this was hardly surprising as motor racing was seen as a high profile way of marketing Fiat products in the USA.

The Grand Prize Race was held at the Savannah circuit in Georgia and Fiat entered three S74s to be driven by Louis Wagner and Americans Caleb Bragg and David Bruce-Brown. The S74 Corsa was a new design based upon the earlier S61 model, with an engine that had been enlarged to 14,137cc but retained the four-cylinder, overhead camshaft configuration. The power output was quoted as 190bhp at 1600rpm and the top speed as 102mph. Also, the S74 retained the side-chain drive of the earlier car. The race was run over 24 laps, totalling 410 miles, and initially saw the Fiats of Bruce-Brown and Bragg take the lead, lapping at 80mph in close company. The big Fiats were very hard on their tyres, enabling Brian Mulford in his Lozier to keep dangerously close. Wagner managed to lap at 80.3mph, but on lap 14 he left the track, damaging the steering and rear axle in the process, resulting in his retirement. Eventually, Mulford, who at the end of the year

Hémery at the 1911 French Grand Prix. (Courtesy NMM)

was declared national driving champion by the American Automobile Association (the AAA), also crashed out. This left Eddie Hearne driving a factory-entered Benz chasing the leading Fiats until near the end of the race when he suffered a puncture that cost him time, but he still managed to hold onto second place, leaving Bruce-Brown the clear winner after over 5½ hours racing. Bruce-Brown's average speed for the race was 74.45mph. Bragg's Fiat, having been passed by Hearne's Benz and de Palma's Mercedes, subsequently finished in fourth place.

A Fiat finished in first place in a 200-mile race in Cincinnati, and a 24-hour race was held in the Los Angeles Motordrome that also saw Fiat victorious. At the Indianapolis 500-mile race, after leading for almost half the race, Bruce-Brown eventually finished in third place. At another event at Indianapolis that year, a Fiat set a new record for a distance of 150 miles; unfortunately once again neither driver nor model of car is recorded. Cuba and Argentina also saw Fiat victorious in certain events. The

Profile of a 1911 S74 Corsa. (Courtesy NMM)

Argentinian event was a race from Rosario to Cordova and back; Fiats took the first three places. A 2175-mile race from St Petersburg to Sebastopol resulted in Fiats taking first and second places. The Fiat archives record an unusual event that took place that year in Japan, when a Fiat 90 HP beat a Curtiss biplane in a match race! Japan had embraced aviation before World War 1, and had acquired a range of aircraft from both Europe and the USA, which included Curtis biplanes. Although it is not recorded, it can be assumed that Baron Okura was involved in the organisation of this event. Finally, in Geneva, Fiats set new one-mile Swiss records in both the racing and touring classes.

With European racing virtually non-existent, Fiat decided to tackle the World Land Speed record. It succeeded in finding a sponsor in the shape of a Russian prince, Boris Soukhanoff. To this end they designed the enormous S76 model, of which two were made. The specially designed engine had four cylinders that totalled 28,352cc and produced some 290bhp at 1900rpm; it had been intended for installation in the Forlanini airship, although it is not certain that this ever happened. Each cylinder had a bore of 190mm and a stroke of 250mm, resulting in a cubic capacity of 7084cc, and had valves operated by overhead camshafts. This huge engine required triple ignition systems for each cylinder and had to be started with compressed air. Due to the height of the car, the radiator cap was 5ft off the ground, and could only be filled if the mechanic stood on the front chassis rails! An innovative feature for Fiat cars of that period was the curvaceous shape of the radiator, which contrasted sharply with the angular designs then prevalent, but became the style adopted for Fiat cars from 1913 onwards.

When road tested in Turin by Felice Nazzaro, he considered the car, now known as the 'Beast of Turin,' to be uncontrollable and, as a consequence, he never drove one again. This huge car belched flames from its exhausts and, it was claimed, could reach 115mph in second gear (it had four gears). One car was taken to Brooklands for the Whit-Monday race meeting where Pietro Bordino drove it round the circuit.

Plan of the S76 300 HP 'Beast of Turin' record breaker. (Courtesy FCA)

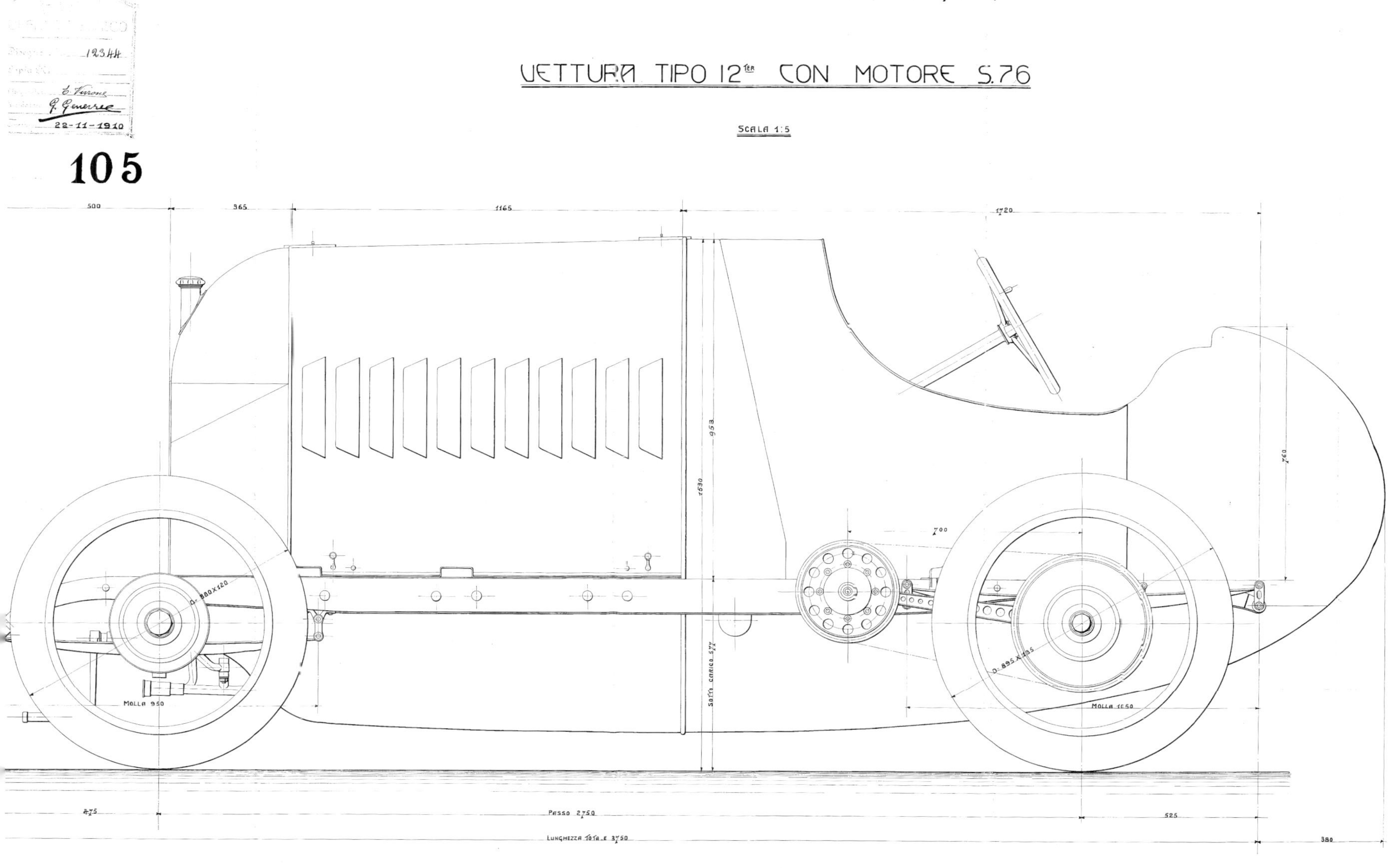

This photograph clearly shows the size of S76. (Courtesy FCA)

It is claimed that he refused to exceed 90mph, although Fiat archives in Turin record that he broke the one-mile record at 121mph. *The History of Brooklands Motor Course* by the late William (Bill) Boddy, generally accepted to be the definitive history of racing/record breaking at the course, makes no mention of such an achievement, although recording the Fiat's presence there. Bordino was accompanied by Soukhanoff for just one lap, which proved to be enough! Following its appearance at the Weybridge venue the S76 became known as the 'Brooklands 300hp.'

After its Brooklands appearance, the car remained in England and next appeared at Saltburn-by-the-Sea, which is on the East coast of North Yorkshire, and boasts some six miles of beach. Due to the length of the sands, it was during 1905 that the first motor race took place there. In addition to races on the sands, record-breaking attempts had also taken place. In 1911 world records for the flying kilometre and flying mile were held by the 21.5-litre 'Blitzen' Benz, and Fiat decided to attempt to break these records with the S76. Rather than have the car transported from Brooklands, Bordino decided to drive it there; this involved a journey of some 250-plus miles on public roads. It has been reported that at times the car exceeded 120mph! At Saltburn, the sands were damp and Bordino 'only' managed to achieve 116mph over the measured mile, which was still a new record. An S76 only appeared once more, this time in 1913 in Belgium, because there was no suitable Italian venue at which a record attempt could take place. Also, Bordino had clearly had enough of the 'Beast of Turin' and so Soukhanoff (who now owned one car) recruited the Belgian-American driver Duray for the record attempt. Based at Ostend, Duray managed to achieve a one-way kilometre speed of 132.37mph, marginally faster than the previous record held by the 'Blitzen' Benz. Unfortunately, bad weather and operational difficulties with the local tramway superintendent, meant that a second run did not take place, and therefore a World Record could not be claimed (since 1910 a mean time based upon two runs was required

Nazzaro and Fagnano aboard the S76. (Courtesy FCA)

FIAT IN MOTORSPORT SINCE 1899

The front (left) and rear (right) of the S76 as seen at the NEC Classic Car Show.

Left and above: The S76 seen at Chateau Impney. (Courtesy PMcF)

to claim a World Record). Of the two S76s built, one remained with Fiat, eventually being destroyed after the First World War, though the engine was retained. In terms of the 'Soukhanoff' car, having passed through Mexico, it eventually arrived in Australia, but with the original engine replaced by an American Stutz engine. Prince Soukhanoff was never seen again after the end of the First World War, and was assumed to be a casualty of the Russian Revolution.

However, the story of the 'Beast of Turin' does not end there, because in 2003 English vintage car enthusiast Duncan Pittaway traced the 'Soukhanoff' car to an Australian motor museum, and managed to purchase it. Basically, it was just a chassis, minus engine, gearbox and body. Then Pittaway learnt that the engine of the other S76 still existed, which was then purchased. The body, gearbox and radiator were recreated using original drawings. In 2015 the S76 re-emerged, and since then has been seen at various events such as Goodwood, Prescott, Chateau Impney, and more. It was also displayed at the NEC Classic Car Show.

1912 saw a limited resumption of Grand Prix racing with the seventh Targa Florio taking place during May. The entry list included six Fiat overhead-valve tourers, two of which finished in third and fourth places behind the winning Scat and the second-placed Lancia. The third place Fiat was driven by Giuseppe Giordano, his average speed being a little over 25mph.

The following month the French Grand Prix took place in Dieppe, organised by the ACF, and, for the first time, included the Coupe de l'Auto for smaller engine cars, and run concurrently. Fiat entered three 14,137cc S74s to be driven by Louis Wagner, David Bruce-Brown and Ralph de Palma. Their main rivals were the 7603cc L76 Peugeots, although much smaller in terms of engine size, and the largest engine entrant, the 15,095cc Lorraine-Dietrich, four of which were entered. It was a two-day event and at the end of the first day Bruce-Brown's Fiat led from Boillot's Peugeot, with Wagner's Fiat in third place. Astonishingly, the next three places were held by 2996cc Sunbeams that were leading the Coupe de l'Auto class. The huge Lorraine-Dietrich quartet was eliminated by mechanical problems. Day two saw problems for the Fiats, as they were dogged with slow tyre changes due to their wooden wheels with detachable rims, rather than Rudge-Whitworth wire wheels. This allowed Boillot to get ahead

FIAT IN MOTORSPORT SINCE 1899

D Bruce-Brown in the S74 at 1912 French Grand Prix. (Courtesy NMM)

D Bruce-Brown waiting to start the second day of the 1912 French GP. (Courtesy NMM)

Wagner in his S74 before the 1912 French Grand Prix. (Courtesy FCA)

in his Peugeot, maintaining the lead to the end of the race. Both Bruce-Brown and de Palma were disqualified for refuelling away from the pits, and Wagner, in the remaining Fiat, finished second. The highest finishing Coupe de l'Auto entrant was the Sunbeam of Resta, which finished in third place overall. This result was the swansong of the giant cars in Grand Prix racing in Europe.

In the USA, however, several S74s had been sold to private owners and achieved some success. During May at Santa Monica, on this occasion driving S61 Corsa models, Teddy Tetzlaff and Caleb Bragg finished first and second, with the former averaging 78.50mph and setting the fastest lap at 90.03mph. The Indianapolis 500 took place at the end of May,

Wagner's car is refuelled. (Courtesy NMM)

and Tetzlaff led for most of the race in his S74, eventually finishing second after having to replace a burst tyre. At Tacoma, driving an S61 instead of the larger S74, Tetzlaff scored a couple of wins. The 1912 Grand Prize Race was held at Milwaukee and a team of three S74s were entered to be driven by Tetzlaff, Bragg and Bruce-Brown. However, tragedy struck when, during practice before the race Bruce-Brown and Anthony Scudelari, his mechanic, were killed. In Bruce-Brown's place, the great Barney Oldfield was substituted, it being his first major race. Tetzlaff led from the start, followed closely by Bragg. However, with some 244 miles of the 410-mile race completed, Tetzlaff's Fiat suffered a broken radius arm. Bragg's Fiat now took the lead, but was hotly pursued by de Palma in a Mercedes. Trying to overtake Bragg, de Palma's car touched wheels with the Fiat and as a result overturned, leaving the former to take victory. Oldfield finished in a creditable fourth place. Another important event was the Vanderbilt Cup, which was held in Milwaukee. Tetzlaff entered, driving one of the smaller S61 models, but, having led for some time, his transmission failed and his sole reward was fastest lap.

Back in Europe, there were several successes in a variety of events. There were class wins in Raid events in Austria and Hungary and also in

Frontal view of Wagner's massive 1912 Fiat.

S57/14B Corsa introduced in 1914. (Courtesy NMM)

the Mont Ventoux Hillclimb. It is not clear which model Fiats took part or whether they were official or private entries, but they are recorded in the Fiat archives in the Turin museum. In Russia a Fiat finished first in the Grand Prix of the Automobile Club of Odessa.

1913 saw a number of regulation changes that effectively outlawed the previous Grand Prix 'giants,' with the result that Fiat did not enter any major events in Europe that year. Whilst developing new models for the new formula, which would also apply in 1914, in the USA, where Fiat had sold a number of the S74 Grand Prix giants, many successes were achieved. In fact, whilst the drivers are not named, the Fiat Museum in Turin lists eight victories in events mainly held in California. The most important of these was in the Los Angeles to Sacramento road race that was won by Frank Verbeck, another Fiat finished in third place, but the name of the driver is not recorded. Also included in the results is a Fiat victory in the Imperial Valley Road Race, again in California.

In Italy, the best Fiat could manage in that year's Targa Florio was fourth place by Giordano. In a speed trial at Vercelli, De Moraes finished first in the touring car class with a time of 31min 3s, which represented a speed of just under 71mph. Elsewhere in Europe victories were recorded in minor events in Austria, Germany, Switzerland and Croatia. In faraway Australia, a Fiat 'Zero' was victorious in a race that went from Sydney to Mudgee and Singleton before returning to Sydney, once again the name of the driver is not recorded. The 'Zero,' or 12-15 HP, was the first small capacity car produced in quantity by Fiat; it was a tourer that was fitted with a four-cylinder inline side valve engine of 1846cc capacity similar to that fitted to the earlier Type 1.

Both Fiat and Mercedes returned to Grand Prix racing in what initially promised to be an exciting year, which unfortunately came to an end in Europe with the outbreak of the First World War on July 28. The one major European event that did take place was the Grand Prix de France, held on a new circuit near Lyon on July 4. A new formula that stipulated a maximum engine size of 4.5 litres and a maximum weight of 1100kg proved to be popular with manufacturers. For this race, and to comply with the new regulations, Fiat had introduced the S57/14B Corsa. This model was powered by a four-cylinder in-line engine of 4492cc capacity; it had overhead valves actuated by overhead camshafts, front wheel brakes, a first for Fiat, plus servo assistance. Another first on a Fiat Grand Prix car was the streamlined tail end that was tapered. 13 teams were entered for the race, one of which was the Fiat team of three cars to be driven by Fagnano, Cagno, and former Fiat mechanic turned driver, Englishman, Jack Scales. However, it was not a glorious return to Grand Prix racing for the team, as only Fagnano finished, having held sixth place for several laps, on the final lap he slipped down the field to last place out of the 11 finishers. The reason for Fagnano's low finish was due to the fact that, during pre-race scrutineering, the Fiat engines were found to be very slightly above the

1914 French Grand Prix – Fagnano in his S57/14B. (Courtesy FCA)

1914 French Grand Prix – Cagno in his S57/14B. (Courtesy FCA)

Waiting for the start of the 1914 French Grand Prix – Fagnano's car nearest to camera.

permitted dimensions of cylinders and, to avoid the embarrassment of disqualification, they were allowed to start, but would be disqualified if they finished amongst the leaders. Cagno only managed to complete 11 of the 20 laps before retiring, whilst Scales, who had been as high as 10th, only managed six laps before he too retired. Much to the disgust of the French crowd, who had eagerly anticipated a win for George Boillot in his Peugeot, the final result was a one-two-three for the Mercedes team, led by Christian Lautenschlager. It had been a very exciting race with Boillot leading for 12 of the 20 laps, only for his car to fail on the last lap. Although the debut of the S57/14B had been somewhat disastrous, its glory days were to come after the First World War.

Before the Grand Prix, in Sicily the ninth Targa Florio had taken place and Luigi Lopez brought his Fiat home in third place. This year's race comprised a single lap of the 651-mile course and Lopez's time was 21h 44min at an average speed of just under 30mph. Despite the fact that it had become very clear Fiat's years of Grand Prix glory were now behind them, several victories were achieved in other European races and in Scandinavia, where Brambeck finished first driving a 30/45 HP model in the 800-mile Gothenburg to Stockholm race. The 30/45 HP was a tourer/cabriolet with a 699cc engine. Two Fiats completed the 1530-mile Circuit of the Carpathians without penalty; similarly three Fiats completed the 1820-mile circuit of the Austrian Alpine Trial without penalty. Also in Austria, Eduardo Weber drove his Fiat to first in class in the hillclimb held at Pyrnpass. In Tuscany, Giorgio won the 'gentleman' category in the Florence Cup. Events held in Russia and Spain also recorded Fiat successes.

So, with a single exception, Fiat's participation in motor racing in Europe came to an end in 1914. However, Bulgaria, which did not enter the First World War until October 1915 (Italy only entered in May of that year), held a 12-mile sprint at Sofia that was won by Savicky in his 50/60hp model. The 50/60 HP model, also known as the Type 5, was a touring car with a 9017cc engine, this model, together with the Type 6 that had a similar sized engine, was the last production car made by Fiat to have an engine capacity exceeding 5000cc.

Further afield, in South America, several victories were obtained by Fiat drivers in races held in Argentina and Chile. In Buenos Aires, Filippini had two race victories, but the model of Fiat used is not recorded, whilst in Valparaiso, Gosch scored a win in his Type 3. The Type 3 was a tourer with a 3967cc engine, also known as the 20-30 HP.

The Heroic Age was now well and truly over, as Europe and the rest of the world became embroiled in the massive tragedy that was the First World War. Perhaps one of the most poignant commentaries on this period of motor racing was written by Lord Montagu of Beaulieu in his 1963 book *The Gordon Bennett Races*. He wrote "But the memory lives on – the memory of immense, slow turning engines, of thrashing chains, of dust clouds which resolved themselves into swaying, bouncing chassis, of brass bands playing national anthems, of puncturing tyres and overheated clutches, of neutralised areas and, above all, of human endurance." Whilst this was in memory of the Gordon Bennett races, it could equally apply to the whole of the 'Heroic Age.' Never again would these massively-engined racing cars be seen at Grand Prix races; the drivers of these machines were heroes by any yardstick.

The Heroic Age Continued – 1906 to 1914

Cagno at speed, before retiring.

Cagno exiting a corner.

A Fiat taking the hairpin bend at Les Sept Chemins in the 1914 French Grand Prix. (Courtesy NMM)

CHAPTER THREE
The Glorious 1920s

Emerging from the chaos of the First World War, during which Fiat had prospered from military contracts, the firm resumed its racing activities as soon as conditions permitted. As a preliminary step, Fiat re-introduced the 1914 S57-based models, and it was with one of these that on July 24, 1919, Ferdinando Minoia set the best time at speed trial on Fanø beach in Denmark. Although based upon the original 1913/14 design, several modifications had been made to the S57, including increasing the engine size to 4859cc, increasing both the wheelbase and track, and improved valve gear, all of which resulted in much better handling and performance; these models were now known as S57/14B.

Antonio Ascari made his first appearance for Fiat when he drove an S57/14B to victory in the 33-mile Parma to Poggio di Berceto hillclimb held on October 5, 1919. His time of 38min 11s represents a speed of 51.75mph. At the same event a young Enzo Ferrari took part in his first competitive motoring event, he finished fourth in his class driving a CMN. On October 19, Ascari finished first in the Consuma Cup hillclimb. He was again driving an S57/14B, and set a time of 13min 38s, representing a speed of 43.72mph.

The tenth annual running of the Targa Florio took place on November 23. The weather was wild and stormy with two days of torrential rain causing havoc on the mountain roads, adding to which mist and hail/snow showers ensured that the race was going to be a true test of man and machine. Fiats had five cars amongst the two dozen entries, including two 1914 Grand Prix models to be driven by Ascari and Count Giulio Masetti. At the start of the race, Ascari roared into the lead, but failed to complete a lap after he skidded into a ravine, where he had to wait to be rescued until the race was over! Masetti

Advertisement for the 501 Sport, note the cigarette!

hung on and eventually finished fourth in this four-lap race. It is believed that Masetti's car was one of the S57 models that had its engine size increased to 4859cc with the intention of participating in the 1917 Indianapolis 500 race (cancelled when the USA entered the First World War). Not having left Italy and being stored at Genoa Docks, these cars were then put up for sale and Count Masetti is believed to have been one of the purchasers.

Fiat's participation in 1920 was once again based on the S57/14B models. On May 20 the Consuma Cup hillclimb took place, and once again saw Fiats victorious, with Paolo Niccolini and Masetti taking first and second places in their class and Emilio Materassi finishing first in the up to 4500cc class. Niccolini's time was 13min 9s, which represented 45.33mph, and Materassi's time was 14min 51s giving a speed of 42.63mph. As in the previous year's event, Fiat was victorious in the Parma to Poggia di Berceto hillclimb, with Masetti at the wheel. His winning time was 38min 28s, which represented a speed of 51.35mph. The eleventh running of the Targa Florio took place on October 24 in very wet conditions. No large engine Fiats were present, but several of the smaller 1500cc-engined 501s were there, and proceeded to take first and second places in their class, and fourth and fifth places overall. These were driven by Giuseppe Piro and Pio Maravigna. The Fiat 501 model represents an important milestone in the company's history; it was the first new postwar design to emerge from any manufacturer, and had the smallest engine of any Fiat up to that time, apart from the very early 1900/1901 models. It was fitted with a four-cylinder, side valve engine of 1460cc giving the basic model a top speed of some 44mph. During its production lifetime from 1919 to 1926, over 45,000 of the basic model were produced. There were several variants, the most notable in terms of competition were the 501S and 501SS models, produced from 1921, which achieved many racing successes in their classes. Due to an increase in power from 23 to 26.5bhp, maximum speed of the side valve 501S rose to 57mph, an increase over the basic model of some 13mph. However, the 501SS with its overhead valve engine with twin overhead cam shafts increased this to 72bhp at 5500rpm, and is variously described as the 802. This engine was, in effect, one half of the new eight-cylinder 801-402 Grand Prix car. Some 2600 were produced.

An event took place in Gallarate on November 14, and Fiats driven by Carlo Conelli and Carlo Sozzi came first and second respectively in their class; which Fiat models they were driving is not recorded. Conelli's time is recorded as 31min 4s, representing a speed of 70.36mph.

Fornaca had taken over as head of technical development in 1909 and had, by now, assembled a group of engineers and designers that were second to none. With the assistance of Carlo Cavalli, who had been a lawyer by profession, but had joined Fiat in 1909, the assembled team included Walter Becchia, Vincenzo Bertarione, Cesare Cappa, Vittorio Jano and Tranquilo Zerbi. Cavalli, despite his legal background, had joined Fiat as a draughtsman in 1905, having gained a degree in mechanical engineering in Turin. Becchia started his career at Fiat, and was partly responsible for the Grand Prix winning 804. He later moved to Sunbeam-Talbot-Darracq (STD) where he was responsible for the Sunbeam that Henry Segrave raced to victory in the 1923 French Grand Prix. His later success included the Lago-Talbots and the humble Citroën 2CV. Bertarione was involved with the design of cars up to the revised 2000cc formula, after which he had little involvement and left to join the Sunbeam-Talbot-Darracq combine where he designed the Grand Prix Sunbeam that appeared to be an almost identical clone of the GP Fiats; when he moved on again he was replaced by Walter Becchia.

Cappa was largely responsible for the 803 and 804 models before moving to Itala, but he did return to Fiat in 1933 when it acquired OM, for whom he was then working. Jano, who subsequently achieved considerable fame at Alfa Romeo, particularly with respect to his design of the P2, worked under Cappa, but after quarrelling with management at Fiat was recruited by Alfa Romeo in 1923. In 1938 he left Alfa Romeo and joined Lancia where, once again he produced some noteworthy designs, not least of which were the V6 Aurelia and the D50 Grand Prix car. Zerbi's greatest achievement was not in cars, but the double-twelve aircraft engine of 1931. He is also remembered for the still-born two-stroke racing engine. However, when Cavalli became ill, Zerbi took control of the car programme and was instrumental in the development of the 508 light car.

The 1921 season started in January with a speed event near Rome, and Masetti set the fastest time. On May 8, the Parma to Poggio di Berceto hillclimb took place, and yet again Fiats were successful. Niccolini took his S57/14B to overall victory, whilst Minoia took his 801/401 to victory in his class, followed by Weber. Niccolini's time for the 32 miles was 35min 39s which equates to an average speed of 53.2mph, while Minoia's time was 43min 21s, averaging

Masetti, winner of the 1921 Targa Florio. (Courtesy FCA)

50.42mph. The 801/401Corsa was Fiat's first postwar Grand Prix car, and its class win in the Parma to Poggio di Berceto event was its first competitive outing. It had a four-cylinder in-line engine of 2973cc to comply with the latest Grand Prix formula; its 16 overhead valves were actuated by twin overhead camshafts and the power output was quoted as 112bhp at 4000rpm giving it a top speed of around 100mph. It wasn't a particularly successful car, only making two appearances, the first being the aforementioned hillclimb, where it won its class, and the Targa Florio.

The 11th Targa Florio took place on May 29, which turned out to be a three-way race between Fiat, Mercedes and Alfa Romeo. In addition to Count Masetti in his S57A/14B, Fiat also entered two of the more up-to-date three-litre 801/401 models, one of which was to be driven by Minoia. The S57A/14B was a development of the S57/14B, with the engine size increased to 4859cc and maximum power to 150bhp. The race turned into an epic duel between Masetti in his Fiat and Max Sailer in his Mercedes. At the end of the first lap Sailer, in the more powerful Mercedes, was in the lead, but to everyone's surprise only by 21 seconds from Masetti. At the end of the second lap, Masetti had taken the lead and had a 2½ minute advantage. However, Sailer fought back and at the end of lap three was only 58 seconds behind Masetti. Masetti now responded and at the finish had a lead of just two minutes and 11 seconds, after 268 miles of racing and over seven hours of driving, averaging 36.13mph. Minoia in the 801/401 finished in eighth place, which, as recorded above, was the last appearance of this model. In 11th place came a 501 driven by Tersilio Bergese – a precursor to the many events that these small Fiats would be seen in, albeit mainly, but not exclusively, national events. Giuseppe Pellegrino finished in 18th place, driving what appears to be a 501.

Florence was the venue for the Coppa delle Cascine held in early June, where Augusto Tarabusi's Fiat was victorious with a time of 1h 13min. Also during June, the Consuma Cup hillclimb saw Fiat record three class wins, with Weber victorious in the up to 3000cc class, Brogliotti in the up to 4500cc class and Luigi Angelini in the larger class; once again the actual models used is not recorded. Angelini's speed was 43.7mph, Brogliotti's 34.4mph and Weber's 39.5mph; it is surprising that Brogliotti, although driving a larger car, was 5mph slower than Weber! August saw Masetti drive his S57/14B to victory in the Susa-Moncenisio hillclimb. During the same month, yet another win took place at Fanø beach in Denmark.

Pellegrino finishing 18th in the 1921 Targa Florio. (Courtesy FCA)

As Grand Prix racing had now resumed, Italy decided to stage its own Grand Prix, in addition to the French race. This took place on September 4 on a circuit near Brescia. For this season the three-litre Indianapolis formula was adopted, and Fiat entered three of its new three-litre 801-402 Grand Prix cars, to be driven by Bordino, Wagner and Ugo Sivocci. The race turned into a contest between Fiat and the French Ballot team, with Bordino leading for Fiat and Goux leading for Ballot. Having led for much of the race, Bordino first suffered a puncture and then had a mechanical failure. The one surviving 801, driven by Wagner, eventually finished in third place having coped with several tyre changes; his average speed for the 322-mile race was 86.9mph. The 801-402 Grand Prix car was basically an 801-401 with the original four-cylinder engine replaced by an eight-cylinder unit of the same size, but the power output increased to 120bhp. This model had a very short Grand Prix career, as for 1922 the formula changed to allow only cars with a maximum engine capacity of 2000cc.

Less than a week later, at an event near Brescia, Niccolini and Count Gaston Brilli-Peri finished first and second respectively in their S57A/14B models. Niccolini's winning time was 20min 3s, and his average speed was 110.22mph. At the same time, in the USA, a 250-mile race near Los Angeles saw a Fiat take first place, though the driver is not recorded.

For the 1922 Grand Prix season the previous three-litre formula was replaced with new regulations that stipulated a maximum engine size of two litres and a minimum weight of 650kg; these regulations remained in place until the end of 1925. Fiat responded to this change with its Tipo 804-404, which had a six-cylinder engine, and largely based on the previous eight-cylinder three-litre Tipo 801. With a capacity of 1991cc, the twin overhead camshaft engine developed 112bhp at 5000rpm. The 804 was the first six-cylinder Grand Prix car that was successful, and its overall design set new standards, especially in regard to its aerodynamically advanced bodywork.

In January, Bordino was in the USA with an 801-401, which was now ineligible to compete in European Grands Prix. He set a fastest lap of 115.90mph and finished fourth at a board track event at Beverley Hills. He was back in the USA in June with the same car, and won a 50-mile race at Northway, Santa Rosa, also in California.

The 1922 Targa Florio took place on April

1922 804-404 Corsa model. (Courtesy FCA)

2, when a Fiat 802 driver by Enrico Giaccone won the 1500cc class at 37.09mph and finished fifth overall. His team-mate, Evasio Lampiano finished 14th, and second in the 1500cc class; he was driving a 501S (or SS as described in some reports).

Before the French Grand Prix, the Parma to Poggio di Berceto hillclimb had taken place during May, and once again Fiats were victorious in several categories. In the 3000 category, Biagio Nazzaro set fastest time in his 801-402 with Brilli-Peri taking third place in a S57A/14B. Nazzaro's time was 35min 41s, which represented a speed of 51.11mph. In the 1500 category, Lampiano and Bergesse were first and second fastest in their 501 models. Lampiano managed to record a time of 37min 40s, and a speed of 49.95mph.

At Mugello on June 1, Gianotti and Cecchi, both driving 501s, finished first and second respectively in the 1500cc class. Gianotti's time for the 240-mile race was 6h 32min, an average speed of 36.40mph. On the June 10, at a meeting at Stockholm, Stjernsvaerd took first place in his 501.

The Coppa delle Faucille took place on July 11 at Gex, close to the Franco/Swiss border not far from Geneva. It was a hillclimb, and the up to 1500cc class was won by Lampiano driving his 501SS (or 802 as it is often called).

Three 804-404 models were entered for the French Grand Prix that was to be held on July 14, on an eight-mile circuit outside Strasbourg. These were to be driven by Nazzaro, Bordino and Biagio Nazzaro, who was Felice Nazzaro's nephew. In the 60-lap race Nazzaro took an immediate lead, but was overtaken on the fifth lap by Bordino, who unfortunately retired after an accident due to a rear axle failure. Nazzaro regained the lead which he held until the end of the race; this turned out to be his last major victory in his long and distinguished career. Nazzaro's average speed for the six-hour, 499-mile race was 79.2mph. However, tragedy struck on the last lap when Biagio Nazzaro crashed, due to a similar failure that had caused Bordino to crash, sadly on this occasion with fatal results.

On September 3, the Gran Premio Vetturette race took place on the newly completed Monza circuit. Measuring just over six miles, the new circuit was initially known as the Circuito di Milano. The 370-mile race was for voiturette cars, and Fiat entered a team of four 803-403 models, to be driven by Bordino, Giaccone, Lampiano and Salamano. The 803-403 had a four-cylinder, overhead camshaft 1486cc engine that was specifically designed for the 'voiturette' category of racing that limited engine size to 1500cc. The result was an overwhelming victory for the Fiats, which filled the first four places headed by Bordino. Bordino's time for the race was 4h 30min, his average speed was 83.28mph, and he also set the fastest lap at 90.15mph. The only other Grand Prix held in 1922 was the Italian Grand Prix which took place on the new Monza circuit one week later, on 10th September, and was over 80 laps giving a race distance of 500 miles. On this occasion Fiat entered three cars to be driven by Nazzaro, Bordino and Enrico Giaccone, who replaced the unfortunate Biagio Nazzaro. The cars were the 804-404 models. Race day was extremely wet and the race itself turned into an extremely boring procession

Bordino in 804-404 at French Grand Prix.

> **PIETRO BORDINO**
> Pietro Bordino was born in Turin on November 22, 1887. He joined Fiat, where his father worked as a mechanic. He quickly became the riding mechanic for Vincenzo Lancia and Felice Nazzaro, whilst still a teenager, and began driving when he was 18 years old. His first competitive drive was at the Chateau Thierry hillclimb in France, which he won. Before the First World War intervened, he drove the infamous Fiat S76, known as the 'Beast of Turin' and declared undriveable by Nazzaro, in England at Brooklands and Saltburn by the Sea.
>
> Following the war, he rejoined Fiat and became an extremely successful Grand Prix driver, winning the Italian Grands Prix in 1921 and 1922 and the Milan Grand Prix in 1927.
>
> Bordino's record of wins does not, however, demonstrate his true abilities. He was such a competent driver that Henry Segrave, the well known English driver and winner of the 1923 French Grand Prix and the 1924 San Sebastian Grand Prix for Sunbeam, described him as "the finest road race driver in the world".
>
> On Fiat's departure from Grand Prix racing, Bordino changed to Bugatti. On April 15, 1928, while practicing for the Targa Florio, he hit a dog, which jammed his steering, causing his car to crash into a river. Tragically he drowned before he could be rescued. He was just 40 years of age.

with Bordino leading from start to finish, followed home by Nazzaro. Bordino's time for the race was 5h 43min, his average speed being 86.92mph and his fastest lap, which was also that of the race, was 91.32mph. Giaccone, driving the third Fiat, failed to complete a single lap, retiring with transmission failure. Due to a large number of pre-race withdrawals, just eight cars started and only three finished. The third finisher was Pierre de Vizcaya driving a Bugatti and he was four laps down on the Fiats at the end of the race.

In Australia, during October, a hillclimb took place on a mountain at Coot-tha, near Brisbane. Local drivers, Saden and Woodhead, finished first and second respectively in both their class and in the overall results in their 10 HP models.

Not content to rest on its laurels, for 1923 Fiat produced the 805-405 Grand Prix car. This had an eight-cylinder engine of 1979cc capacity, which was supercharged. This boosted power to 130bhp at 5500rpm. The team's first outing was at the French Grand Prix which was held at Tours this year. Having led for much of the race, the cars ultimately retired due to the ingress of stones and dirt into the superchargers as a result of the poor condition of the circuit's surface. However, the cars had shown remarkable speed with Bordino reaching 122mph on the straight section of the course and he had also lapped at 88mph before retiring. Part of the reason for the 805's pace was the utilisation of a supercharger which was allowed due to an oversight in the regulations drawn up before the First World War. Fiat was one of the first teams to exploit this omission, although Mercedes had designed a supercharged car for the 2-litre formula, but were still banned from Grands Prix. Consolation came for Great Britain in the fact that the race was won by Henry Segrave driving a Sunbeam, the engine of which was considered to be a copy of the 1922 Fiat 804-404. Segrave was the first Englishman ever to win a Grand Prix.

Before the French Grand Prix, the annual Parma to Poggia di Berceto hillclimb took place and saw yet another Fiat win, this time Count Brilli-Peri led team-mate Niccolini to victory, both driving S57A/14B models. Brilli-Peri's time for the 32 miles was 35min 26s, which represented a speed of 53.47mph.

During June the Gran Premio Vetturette was held near Brescia. The 325-mile race lasted for over four hours and the victor was Cagno driving a Tipo 803-403; he averaged 80.34mph and also set the fastest lap at 86.86mph.

On 9th September the first-ever European Grand Prix took place at Monza. This title was thereafter granted to national Grands Prix as an honorary title and the first event to be given this was the Italian Grand Prix. For this race Fiat fitted a different type of supercharger, the previous Wittig vane-type having been replaced by a Roots-type that proved to be less prone to damage by stones, dirt, etc. This modification also gave a power boost, in that the previous output of 130bhp was increased to 140bhp. This alteration clearly paid off as Carlo Salamano won, followed by Nazzaro. Salamano took 5h 27min to complete the 497-mile race, averaging 91.05mph, and also set the fastest lap

Salamano in 803-403 at Milan voiturette race in 1922. (Courtesy FCA)

Nazzaro in 804-404 at the 1922 Italian Grand Prix. (Courtesy FCA)

Line-up of 1923 team of 805-405 Corsa Grand Prix cars and drivers. (Courtesy FCA)

Salamano's car in the pits at the 1923 European Grand Prix. (Courtesy FCA)

of the race at 98.83mph. The Centro Historico has a copy of a poster celebrating this victory.

In England, at Brooklands, Ernest Eldridge took his Fiat SB 4 special, in its pre-'Mephistopheles' form, to victory in the 18th Lightening Short Handicap race and was rewarded with the Brooklands Founders Gold Cup for his efforts. This was Eldridge's final victory in the elderly Fiat in this form, as shortly afterwards, at another Brooklands event, the engine exploded! But the car was far from dead and eventually emerged as the much modified 'Mephistopheles.' 'Mephistopheles' exists today and is resident in the Fiat museum at Corso Dante in Turin. The story of this remarkable vehicle does have some contentious facts surrounding it. It is claimed that this is the car that Nazzaro drove at Brooklands in the 1908 Fiat/Napier challenge match and that it was subsequently purchased by Sir George Abercromby for £1250. In 1910, Abercromby used the car to lap Brooklands at 106.38mph; apparently several drivers had tried the car but found it a 'handful.' The car then apparently languished unused until 1921 when it was

Poster celebrating 1923 European Grand Prix victory. (Courtesy FCA)

Abercromby in 'Mephistopheles' at Brooklands in 1910. (Courtesy NMM)

discovered in a Fulham mews by John Duff, who purchased it for £100. Duff had been racing a 1908 Fiat S61 with some success, but towards the end of 1921 had sold the S61 to Philip Rampon and acquired 'Mephistopheles.' He managed to lap Brooklands at 106.88mph and a standing lap at 91.52mph. Early in 1922 'Mephistopheles' returned to Brooklands with new pistons, following an engine overhaul, but having lapped at 107.01mph, the engine then proceeded to destroy itself.

Duff then decided to sell the car and Ernest Eldridge bought it for £25. Eldridge set about modifying what had been an SB 4; apparently he sawed the frame in half and extended it by 16in to accommodate the new engine he had acquired. The engine, purchased from a war-surplus store in London, was an enormous 21,706cc overhead camshaft Fiat A12 designed for airships, with a 300 plus bhp power output. When it was first seen at Brooklands, it was still a bare chassis with two seats situated over the rear axle. However, by November it had set a new world record for a standing start half-mile at 77.68mph. Eldridge's ambition was to set a new world land speed record, which he duly did in 1924. On 12th July, at Arpajon in France, he set a new world land speed record of 146.01mph. He lost his record to Malcolm Campbell on 24th September when Campbell set a new record at 146.16mph at Pendine Sands, South Wales. Campbell's car was a 350bhp V12 Sunbeam. Eldridge continued to race the car, and during 1925 lapped

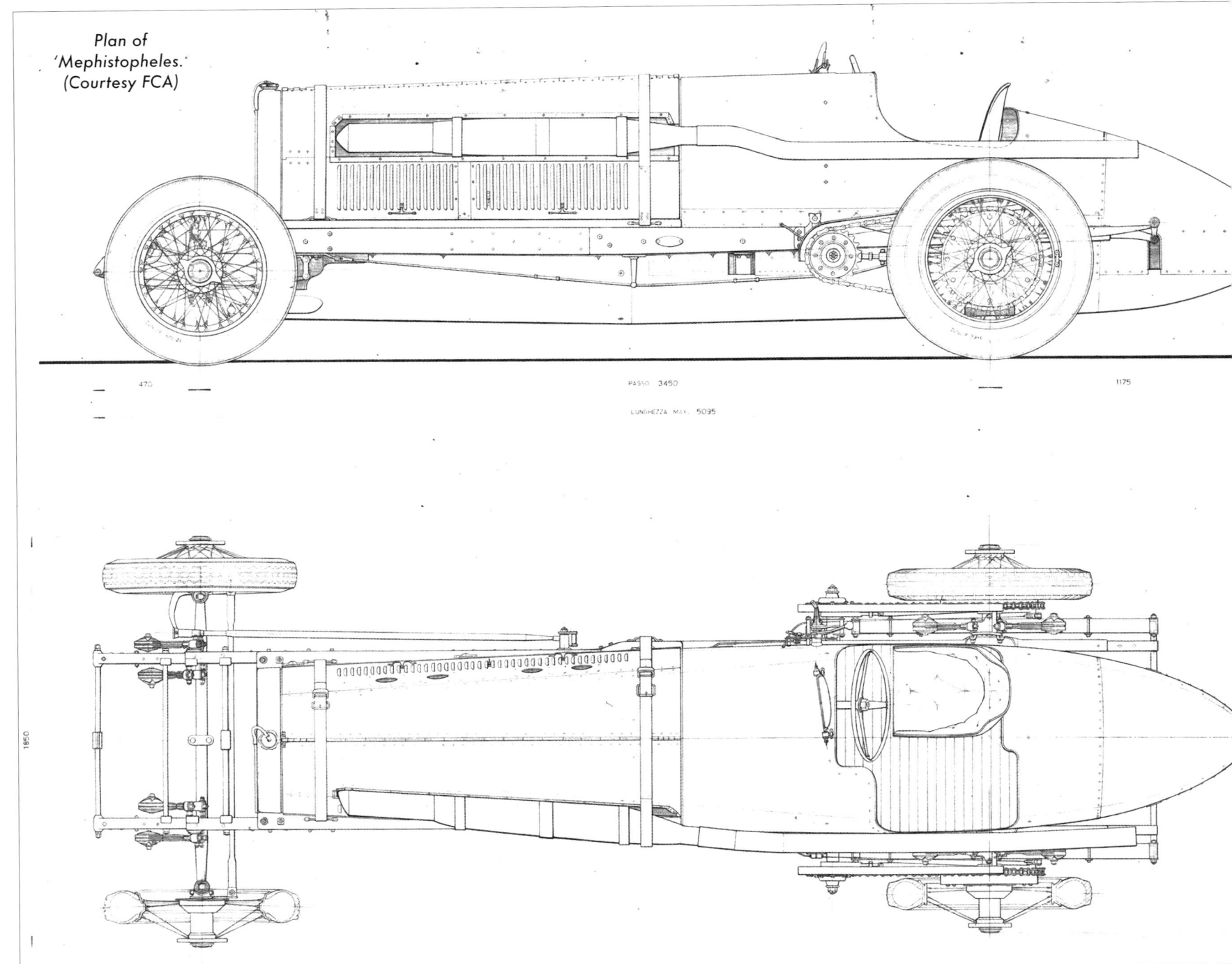

Plan of 'Mephistopheles.' (Courtesy FCA)

Brooklands at a stunning 125.45mph. The car was then sold, but gradually faded away, until, fairly recently, it was acquired by Fiat and is now on display at the Centro Historico in Turin.

Fiats also scored a first and second at an event at Casablanca in Morocco and a victory in a race (or was it a Raid?) over 300 plus miles between Novgorod and Moscow.

The 1924 Grand Prix season in Europe started with the French Grand Prix at Lyons on August 3, and Fiat entered a team of four 805-405 cars, with drivers Bordino, Nazzaro, Cesare Pastore and Onesimo Marchesio. Having been as high as second, Bordino retired with defective brakes and Nazzaro later retired with similar problems, leaving the Alfa Romeo P2 of Ascari as the victor. Marchesio retired with engine problems and Pastore crashed; as a result all four Fiats failed to finish the race. Following this disappointing result, Fiat withdrew from racing for the time being.

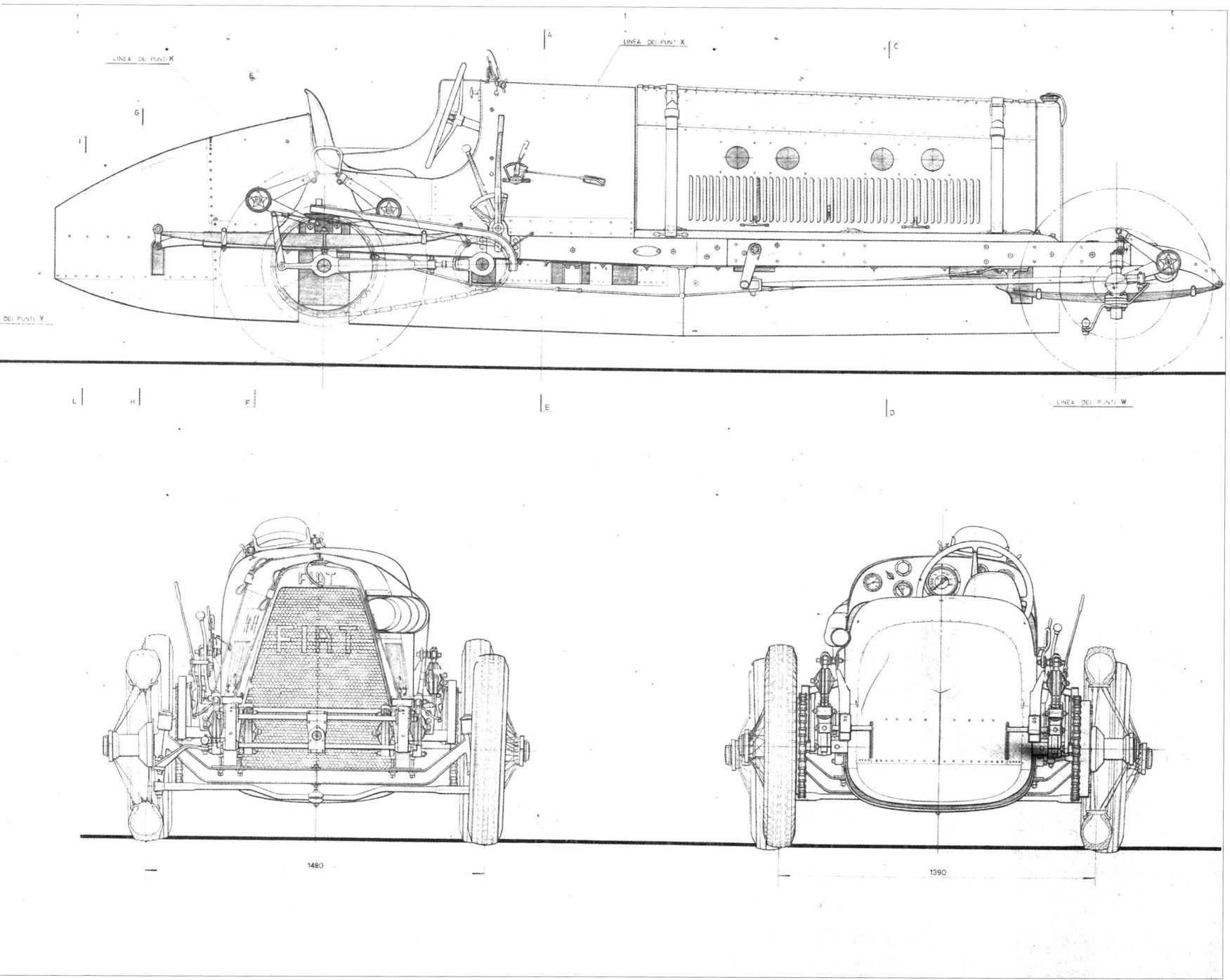

Before this decision, however, Fiat had officially entered two Tipo 803 models in the Targa Florio to be driven by Salamano and Bordino. The 803 model had been introduced in 1921, but had been fitted with a supercharger during 1923, thus attempting to keep it competitive in the voiturette class. Sadly, Salamano crashed in practice, luckily he wasn't seriously injured, but a replacement driver was required. Nazzaro was approached, but declined, as he felt that driving such a fast car on this dangerous circuit was beyond him. Thus, Fiat decided that just Bordino should take part in the Tipo 803 car and that he would be accompanied by a test driver, Pastore, driving a racing version of the Tipo 519 touring car. The race was won by Werner in a Mercedes. Bordino was still suffering from injuries that he had sustained at Monza and collapsed through exhaustion at the pits and so Nazzaro was pressed into service. Nazzaro then crashed, overturning the car, but fortunately

Eldbridge in 'Mephistopheles' in 1923. (Courtesy FCA)

Below and opposite: 'Mephistopheles' as it can be seen today – full view, frontal view, rear view, and the engine.

ORIGINI
FIAT

9
61
X-D
7117
226

FIAT
FIAT

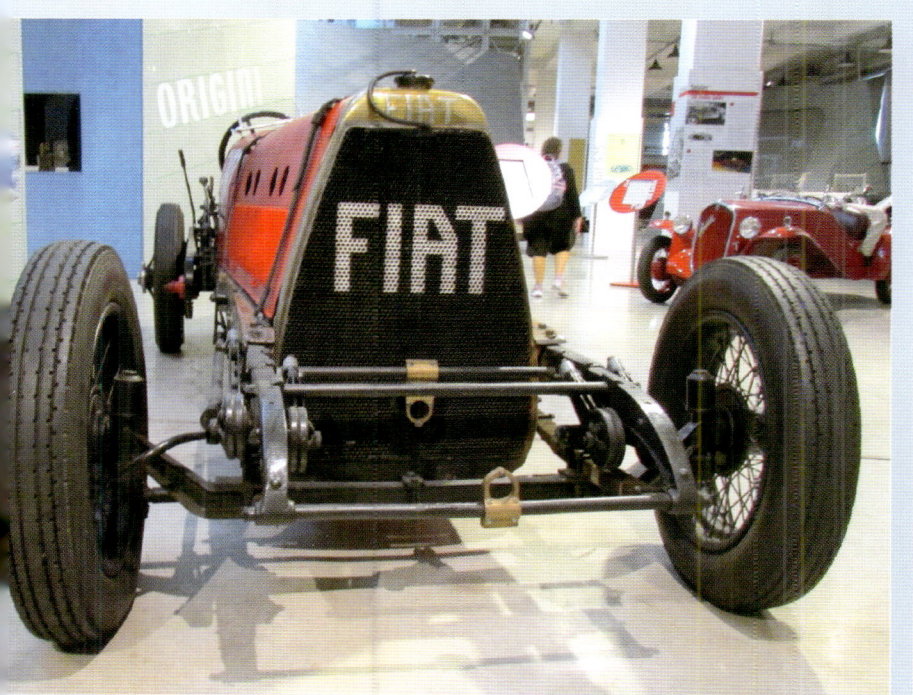

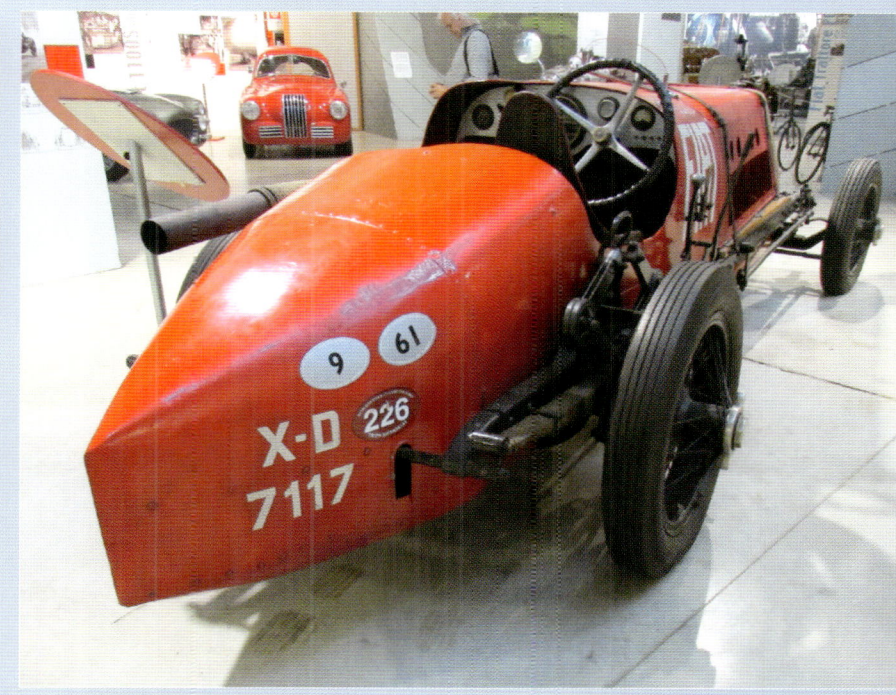

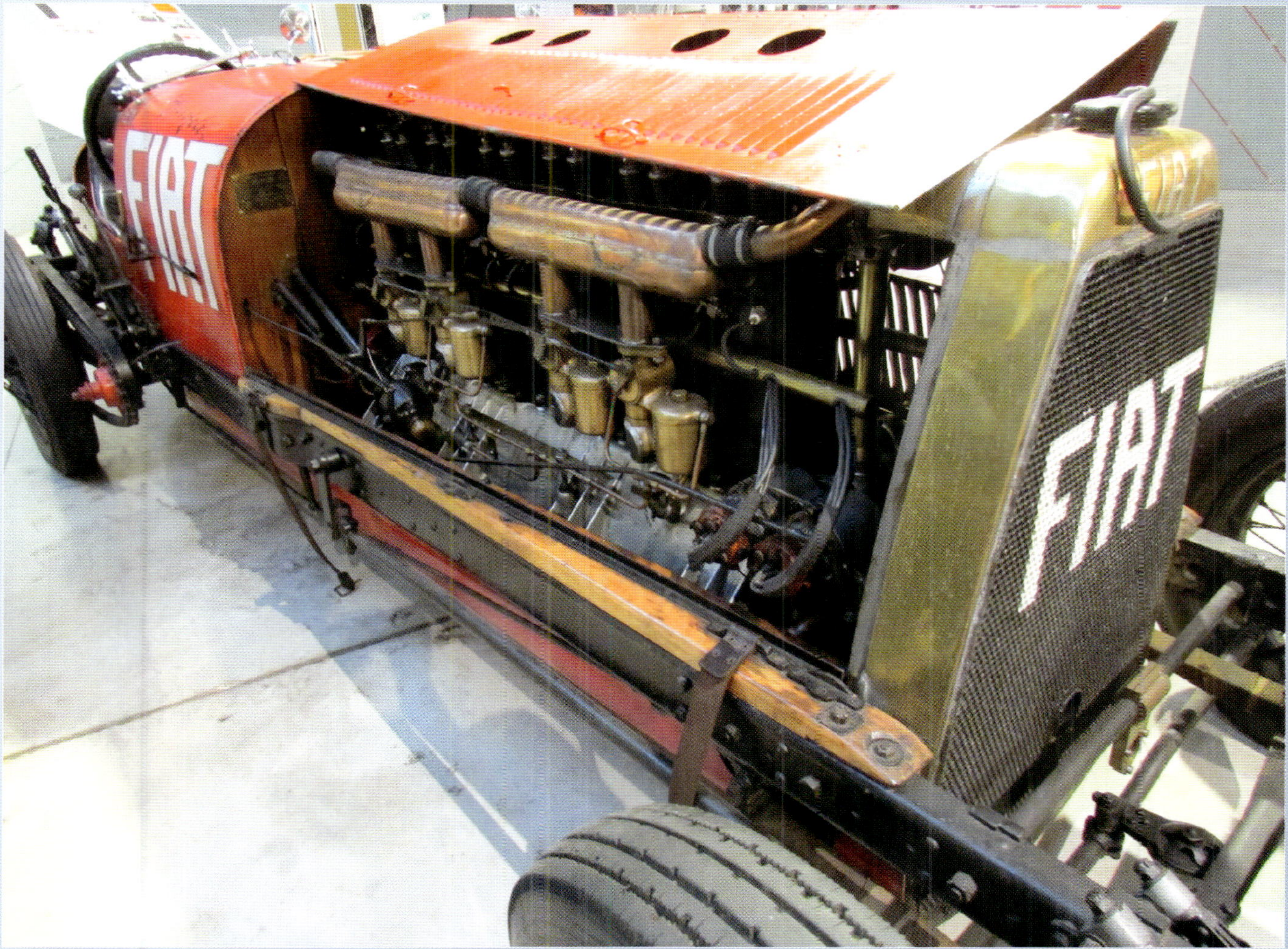

Bordino at the 1924 Targa Florio. (Courtesy NMM)

Another view of Bordino at the 1924 Targa Florio. (Courtesy NMM)

without too much damage to either himself or the car; Bordino then resumed and managed to reach the finish in third place, having averaged 39.6mph over the 268 miles.

As usual, Fiats recorded many successes in lesser events around Europe and beyond. Wins were recorded at the Uruguayan side of the River Plate, at a record-breaking session at Arpajon in France, and at an event in the Eifel mountains in Germany. Nearer to home a seven-mile hillclimb between Biella and Oropa saw Casteldelli take first place in the up to 3000cc class in a time of 11min 17s, giving an average speed of 42.63mph. At Alessandria in April, Fiats scored a remarkable one to five finish in the sports category of an event; further details are not recorded. In August a 242-mile race was held on the Mugello circuit near Florence, where Augusto Tarabusi finished first in the up to 3000cc class after over 6½ hours racing at an average speed of 37.16mph. A 155-mile winter regularity trial took place at Gallarate outside Milan during December, and Elio Scampini finished first in the up to 3000cc class. Unfortunately, the Fiat archive does not specify which model/s were used in these events.

1925 saw a much reduced list of events that Fiat took part in. In a 24-hour race in Denmark, Fiats took first and second places, while in Libya Fiats featured in the first running of what was to become the Tripoli Grand Prix. Libya had been 'colonised' by Italy in 1911 and the occupiers had organised several sporting events, such as regattas, tennis tournaments, camel racing and football championships. In March 1925 a motoring 'raid' had taken place over the Tripolitan interior in which Fiats featured strongly, finishing in the top three places. It is assumed, although not proven, that this led to the organising of the first 'Circuit of Tripolitania' that eventually became the Tripoli Grand Prix. The first race for motorcycles took place on April 15, and on the next day the first of the two car events was held. The first car race was for larger vehicles with an engine capacity that exceeded 2000cc. There were only five entrants: three Fiats, one Lancia and one Cottin-Desgouttes. In the actual race, two of the Fiats retired, but a Fiat 3A driven by Lieutenant Alberto Trivero won, averaging just over 46mph for the 130-mile race. The Fiat 3A could hardly be described as a racing car, but was an open tourer with a 4400cc engine, and

A 1925 model 501S. (Courtesy NMM)

the series became very popular with the armed forces. It was the 3As that had successfully completed the March raid. The following day the race was for cars with an engine of under 2000cc, which attracted a larger field of ten cars, including three Fiat 501S models with only 1460cc engines. The results were not that favourable for the Fiats this time, with two cars finishing in fourth and fifth (last) places. In Sweden a winter race near Stockholm resulted in the first five places taken by Fiats. A 1500cc class win was achieved at Aosta, and, at the Coppa del Garda regularity event of some 215 miles, Pagani took victory in the 1100cc class, driving a 990cc 509, and Castiglioni took victory in the 1500cc class driving a 501SS. Fiats also finished second and third in the smaller class.

The 509 has been described as Fiat's first mass-produced small car, with over 90,000 being produced between 1925 and 1929. It could be had in a number of different configurations and also several high-performance versions, the S and SM variants. The basis of the car was its 990cc, four-cylinder, overhead camshaft engine that in the the S and SM versions produced 27 and 30bhp respectively, an increase of at least 5bhp over the standard model. The S model was normally fitted with a two-seat, boat-tailed body, whilst the SM had a competition body. SM stood for 'Spinto Monza' or Monza Special. The SM was available in two versions, normal and 'Florio Cup,' the latter having a further power boost to 35bhp. There were a few models described as SC, due to their having a supercharger

The results of the 1925 Targa Florio did not include any Fiat successes, but the event was particularly poignant for Fiat. Count Giulio Masetti, who had won the 1921 race for Fiat, died when he crashed in his Delage. In May, Bordino had taken a Tipo 805 to the USA and entered several board track events, plus the Indianapolis 500. In the latter event he finished in tenth place. At Culver City in March he was ninth, but in April he won a 25-mile sprint, averaging 133mph. Similarly to 1923, a Fiat driven by Cagno took part in the event in the Concosso Panrusso, an event organised by the Soviet Government in Russia. The purpose behind this 3360-mile drive from Leningrad (now St Petersburg) and Tiflis (now Tbilisi), was to assess the suitability of various makes for the Soviet Government, and it attracted an enormous amount of interest from manufacturers. Fiat entered two 519s, one for Cagno, two 510s and two 505F lorries. Cagno collected the trophy for the best individual performance and also the fuel-consumption award. This was the 519's only significant competition success, but it was to no avail as the Soviets chose Packards and Lincolns. This was Cagno's final achievement after his long successful career.

Fiat's absence from competition continued through 1926, though private entries achieved some success. In Germany, a race from Cologne to Trier and back to Cologne via Koblenz, saw Fiats victorious in four categories, although the models and drivers are not recorded. At Monza, in the 130-mile Coppa Fiera di Milano race, which included a maximum fuel load, Fiat filled the first four places in their class. This event was held in conjunction with the International Motor Show, which itself was a component of the Milan International Trade Fair, as a means of demonstrating Italian technological achievements with respect to the motor car.

Another Fiat first place was achieved at a regularity event in Germany, and in August Manci and Bertarelli came first and third in the Stelvio hillclimb. Benigni took class honours in his 509S at the Targa Abruzzo, and in Poland a Fiat finished first in a 1km sprint. Once again in Tripoli, Trivero entered his trusty 3A in the large class of the Circuit of Tripolitania, but on this occasion without success, as he retired at the halfway stage. There were no other Fiats entered. The classes had now been redefined, the larger class now being for cars with engines exceeding 1500cc, rather than 2000cc as previously.

For the 1926 and 1927 Grand Prix seasons, the existing two-litre formula was replaced with one that allowed a maximum engine size of 1.5 litres, with a minimum weight of 600kg in 1926, increasing to 700kg for 1927. Another significant change was that there was no longer a requirement to carry a mechanic, so the era of single seat Grand Prix cars had arrived. Despite its earlier decision to quit racing, Fiat developed new designs for the revised formula. The first of these was a six-cylinder two-stroke of revolutionary design, comprising 12 opposed pistons, two geared crankshafts and a Roots-type supercharger. Eventually it produced 152bhp, but by that time the straight-eight Delage Grand Prix car was producing 170bhp, and so the two-stroke project was dropped. Instead, Fiat designers produced the sensational Tipo 806/406. Being a low slung single-seater, it had a twelve-cylinder engine that consisted of two blocks of six cylinders in parallel on a common crankshaft housing, although each block had its own crankshaft. There were three overhead camshafts, the central one for inlet valves and the other two outer ones dealt with the exhaust valves. It had a Roots-type supercharger and a power output of 187bhp, all of which gave the car a reputed top speed in excess of 150mph, considerably higher than the opposition at that time. Early testing showed that the new engine was fragile. For its first, and, sadly, what proved to be its only outing, one was entered for the Gran Premio di Milano, a non-championship race at Monza on the same day as the 310-mile European Grand Prix. The race was run in four heats with a 31-mile final. The weather on the day was atrocious with continuous heavy rain. Having won his heat, Bordino then raced to an easy win despite the very wet conditions, setting the fastest lap during the race. His time for the race was 19min 42s at an average speed of 94.67mph, his fastest lap was 96.61mph. He finished over half a minute ahead of the next finisher, Campari in an Alfa Romeo. It is rumoured that the 806 had been built without Agnelli's knowledge, and that he was so furious at the amount of work involved at a time of economic depression that he ordered the car to be destroyed, along with the 804 and 805 models. As a result the Fiat entry for the British Grand Prix of three 806s was subsequently withdrawn. So, sadly, none of these remarkable Grand Prix Fiats still exist! Allegedly, Agnelli felt that there was now more prestige to be gained from the aircraft sector, where, in particular, success in events such as the Schneider Trophy races gained international recognition and prestige for the country. Never again did a Grand Prix car

A 509 competing in the 1926 Colle della Maddalena hillclimb. (Courtesy FCA)

The revolutionary 806 Corsa. (Courtesy FCA)

bearing the Fiat badge appear, the closest it came was when Fiat owned Ferrari, although the cars were clearly branded 'Ferrari.'

The first Mille Miglia race took place on March 26-27, when Fiat secured two class wins. In the 5000cc class, Silvani and Minozzi took their 519S to victory, and in the 1100cc class, Moalli and Ferrari came first in their 509 model; in both these classes Fiats also finished second. It is interesting to note that the overall winner, Minoia, driving an OM Tipo 665 Sport, completed the 1019 miles in 21h 4min, setting an average speed of 48.27mph, whereas the leading Fiat, the 509S of Moalli took no less then 24h 23min at an average speed of 41.77mph. The race was a truly rigorous test of strength and stamina! The 519S was an uprated edition of the 519, it had the same 77bhp engine of 4766cc, but improvements to the state of tune increased maximum speed from 72mph to 77mph. It was also noted for its large v-shaped radiator, as distinct from the normal flat style. A 509 won the 2300-mile Coppa Agnelli Rally, taking 88 hours to do so. In a tough marathon

Bordino in an 806 at the 1927 Milan Grand Prix. (Courtesy NMM)

Waiting for the start of Heat 1 of the 1927 Milan Grand Prix. (Courtesy NMM)

staged in Romania, a Fiat 509 was one of the six cars that finished unpenalised. Fiats took the first two places in the Coppa Crespi run at Monza, and in the 106-mile Coppa Sila race at Cosenza held in June, a Fiat finished first in its class. The Targa Abruzzo race for touring cars was held on the Pescara circuit on the same day as the Targa Acerbo, which was for racing cars. Spaniard Antonio Zanelli won the 1100cc class in his 509.

The impact of Fiat's withdrawal from front line racing is very evident in the paucity of race records in the archives in Turin for the years 1926 and 1927. In fact, from that period onwards no official records exist and other sources have had to be used.

While Fiat was no longer involved in Grand Prix racing, it wasn't completely absent from motor racing. In the hands of private owners, models such as the 509S were frequently seen in local and national events, and many successes achieved. An example of this was the 1928 Targa Florio race when two 509s took part in the Junior race, unfortunately on this occasion without success as both retired. However, an example of successful participation came in that year's Monte Carlo Rally when two 509A models finished first and second overall. Starting from Bucharest (there were 11 different starting points) Jacques Bignan survived a cracked cylinder block, missed a ferry, and at one point need a team of horses to pull his car out of mud, to finish first. His luck held out though for, as he crossed the finishing line, his magneto failed! E Malaret, also driving a 509A, finished second overall, while Bon, also driving a 509A, finished 11th and Murray brought his 508 into 18th place. In that year's Mille Miglia, once again, a Fiat 509S

Bordino on his way to victory in the 1927 Milan Grand Prix. (Courtesy NMM)

Jacques Bignan on his way to victory in the 1928 Monte Carlo Rally.

driven by Gilera, won its class, despite only finishing 28th overall. Fiats appeared again in Libya for the fourth Tripoli race, which now had the grand title of Gran Premio di Tripoli. There were two entries, one in each class. The type of Fiat entered in the larger class is not recorded, but in the smaller class a 509SC was entered to be driven by Eugenio Riccioli. In the event, Zaitti driving the larger Fiat retired, but Riccioli finished third in his class. This was the last time that a Fiat competed in Tripoli as henceforth the race was for proper Grand Prix cars or, later, voiturette cars.

Despite its anti-competition policy, Fiat entered a team of works-prepared 525S models in the 1929 Alpine Cup trial. These were to be driven by Nazzaro, Salamano and Pastore. They were up against tough opposition from the supercharged Mercedes-Benz driven by Rudolph Caracciola and Werner. Unfortunately, Nazzaro was involved in an accident with a farm cart, and so Fiat was excluded from the team event. Some consolation for the team came from Salamano achieving the fastest time on the Stelvio Pass. Both Salamano and Pastore received Glacier Cups for their efforts. It is said that Fiat's reason for entering this event was to test the effectiveness of its version of the Lockheed hydraulic brake. The 525SS was a more highly developed version of the standard 525 model, a luxury vehicle available in different formats; it had a six-cylinder 3729cc engine with a top speed of 75mph and a power output of 88.5bhp.

The 1929 Mille Miglia had the by now usual phalanx of Fiats entered: there were no fewer than 24 entries, of which three failed to start and 10 failed to complete the course, leaving 11 finishers. The majority of these entries were 509S models, but the highest placed finisher was Ambrosini, driving what was described as a 'Fiat Siata 521 Coupé.'

The 521 was a development of the earlier 520 model, powered by a six-cylinder side valve 2510cc engine that developed 50bhp. It was produced in a variety of configurations including the 521C that had a shortened wheelbase. Over 20,000 examples of the 521 were manufactured, and presumably the Siata version had the benefit of a more highly tuned engine. Ambrosini finished in 25th place overall and in his class, he was followed in to 26th place by Tamburi, who was first in his class, in a 509S. The next three places

525SS on display in Centro Historico.

were also taken by 509S drivers. Siata (Societa Italiano Auto Trasformazioni Accessori) was an Italian car-tuning workshop established in 1926. Before the Second World War it had specialised in modifying cars manufactured by Fiat, but after the war it started manufacturing complete cars under its own name.

In the 1929 Mont Ventoux hillclimb in France, Paul Bablot won his class, while Bignan scored an outright win in the Le Touquet Rally.

So the 1920s drew to a close. It had started with Fiat being at the forefront of Grand Prix racing, having introduced a number of very technically advanced cars, and finished on a much quieter note, having withdrawn from frontline motor racing for ever. But as the next chapters will demonstrate, the Fiat name was never far away from motorsport in many different guises.

CHAPTER FOUR
1930s-1940s: A Quieter Period

Following the wonderful achievements of earlier decades, the 1930s and 1940s were a much quieter period for Fiat in major motorsport events. However, that is not to say they were totally absent from the race track. In the hands of private owners, smaller Fiats participated in numerous national and international events; usually they were in the running for class wins rather than outright victories. Obviously the Second World War resulted in no motor racing from 1940 to 1945, apart from the 1940 Mille Miglia and the 1940 Targa Florio, both of which will be reported on later in this chapter.

The fourth Mille Miglia took place on April 12, 1930, seeing Fiats victorious in two classes. In the 1100cc class a 509S driven by Perccioli finished 31st overall and first in class, similar cars also finished second and fourth, and in the 'utility' class 514s were first and second, with the first place finisher, Mazza, also finishing 42nd overall. The standard 514 was a saloon powered by a 1438cc side valve engine; this model replaced the earlier 509; in addition to the standard model there were several sports

A team of 525SS models at the 1930 Coppa delle Tre Venezia. (Courtesy FCA)

versions, the S, MM and CA models. MM stood for Mille Miglia and CA for Coppa delle Alpi (Alpine Cup). All three sports versions offered more power: the S had 34.5bhp which was 6.5bhp more than the Standard, while the MM and CA versions both had 37bhp. There was also an overhead valve conversion available from Siata. Total production of all versions was 36,970, so it was clearly a popular model, and the sports versions were regularly seen at motor races such as the Mille Miglia.

In the Coppa delle Tre Venezia Alpine Rally held in July, Fiat entered a team of 525SS models, plus some 514s. Despite Nazzaro's rapid pace he finished fourth in his class, but Fiat's honour was upheld by Costa who was the outright winner in his 514S and the utility class was won by a standard 514.

For the 1931 Mille Miglia, the factory offered free preparation and pit services for privately entered 514s. Rumour had it that Fiat was entering three supercharged 514s to be driven by Salamano, Pastore and Nazzaro. In the event no supercharged 514s appeared, although there were significant numbers of privately entered 514s, 525s and 509s. The highest placed Fiat was the 525SS driven by Gilera and Manzoni into 18th place overall and second in class. In terms of the 514s, Di Liddo and Ricceri brought in their 514Spider Sport to 23rd place overall, but first in class. The best performance by a 509 was by Basagni and Scatragli who finished last in 57th place and fourth in class. The entry list for that year's Targa Florio listed two 509s, but one failed to start and the other only completed five laps before retiring. The Alpine Trial saw Dr Armand Lettich win a Glacier Cup in his 522. The 522 was a saloon with a six-cylinder 2516cc engine. It was made in two versions, the C and L, both of which were saloons. Its notable feature was the provision of synchromesh on the two highest gears; over 6000 examples were produced between 1931 and 1933.

1932 was a significant year for Fiat. At the Milan Show Fiat launched its 'car for Europe,' the

514s ready for the 1930 Coppa delle Tre Venezia. (Courtesy FCA)

Tipo 508. The new car was based upon the 509A principle; that is, a compact car with a 995cc side valve engine that produced 20bhp. Whilst the side-valve configuration was not unusual at that time, the almost square dimensions of 65mm x 75mm of the engine certainly were. Most similar sized cars at that time had a piston stroke of at least 85mm, resulting in higher piston speeds. It was called the 'Balilla' after a Genoese boy hero, who allegedly started the revolt against the Austrian occupation of Genoa in the 18th century, but also unfortunately attracted unwelcome attention as the name 'Balilla' was also used for a Fascist Youth group. The late Fiat aficionado, Michael Sedgwick, considered that the most appropriate translation of 'Balilla' was 'the plucky little one'! With modifications such as an overhead-valve cylinder head it proved to be extremely tunable.

During 1932, a sports version, the 508S, the 'Balilla Sport,' was introduced, this was lightly tuned but was clothed in an attractive two-seater spider body with flared wings and a vestigial tail fin. There were two versions, the Coppa d'Oro (Gold Cup) model with sweeping front wings that merged into running boards, or the 'Mille Miglia' model that had cycle front wings. The early editions still had the side-valve engine with three forward gears, but tuned to give 30bhp. Later editions had an overhead-valve engine by Siata that produced a minimum of 36bhp and was accompanied by a four-speed gearbox. Siata also produced a supercharged version of its overhead valve engine that was reputed to have a power output of 48bhp and a top speed of 93mph. By 1934 the basic model was fitted with four forward speed gears as standard. Balillas were popular in Britain as well as elsewhere, as can be seen from the photograph on page 69 of a 508 at a hillclimb at Lewes in 1938.

Today 'Balillas' appear regularly at historic motoring events and we can appreciate the attractiveness of these sporting Fiats of the 1930s.

That year's Mille Miglia attracted the usual horde of Fiat models, 514s and 509s. A 514 MM driven by Gilera and Sartori finished first in its class, whilst in the smaller class the highest placed Fiat was the 509S driven by Losa and Rangoni, who finished second behind a Maserati 1100. The Targa Florio was now reverting to its original philosophy of encouraging entries from Grand Prix teams and this year the race, on the new shorter 'Piccolo Circuito Madonie' was dominated by Alfa Romeo 'Monza' cars, Bugattis, and Maseratis. Tazio Nuvolari, driving a 'Monza' Alfa Romeo, duly won. The entry list did include some touring cars, including two Fiats driven by DeMaria and Sciandra, but neither featured in the final results.

The 1933 Monte Carlo rally took place in

Poster for Coppa delle Tre Venezia.

FIAT IN MOTORSPORT SINCE 1899

508 Balilla Sport in Centro Historico.

A Balilla Sport in a garage/workshop; venue and date unknown. (Courtesy FF)

January. Prince Narischkine, who had started from Tallinn, drove his 508 Balilla into eighth place overall, and third overall in the light car class. The diminutive 508 Balillas faced strong competition in the Mille Miglia from the English MG team in their supercharged Magnettes, and the Maserati team. The result was a comprehensive class win for the MGs, but Ambrosini and Menchetti finished in third place in their Siata-modified Balillas. The 'utility' class was won by Ricci and Maggi driving a standard Balilla Sport.

This year saw the first running of the Czechoslovak 1000-mile race. In the up to 1100cc class, a Walter 'Junior S' driven by Jindrich Knapp finished first in class, but also second overall. The Walter Junior was a 508 Balilla built under licence in Czechoslovakia. Although a team of three 508s took part in that year's International Alpine Trial, they were once again beaten by MGs and, on this occasion, Singers. In the Coppa Acerbo, the highest placed 508 was, yet again, beaten by an MG K3 and also three Maseratis.

In the 1934 Mille Miglia, Gilera and Manzoni, driving a Siata 508S, finished third in class and 14th overall, having been beaten by an 1100cc Maserati and an 1100cc MG, Magnette K3, both of which were far more powerful than the Fiat. In that year's Czechoslovak 1000-mile race Walter Juniors took second, fourth and fifth places in the up to 1100cc class.

Numerous class victories were achieved by the 508S model, among the most important were the Giro d'Italia, the Belgian Ten Hours and the Klausen and Harmashatar hillclimbs. Also a 508S was driven into third in class in the 24 hours race at Le Mans

January 1935 saw the 14th Monte Carlo Rally, and a Fiat driven by Husem and Larsen, starting from Stavanger, and finishing tenth overall and third in class. In terms of rallies, Mme Dubac-Taine came fifth in the Paris to St Raphaël Rallye Féminin, Stothert received a first-class award in the RAC Rally, and Pilloud scored a class win in the Circuit des Vosges mountain rally.

Second in class was the best result for Fiat in the 1935 Mille Miglia, the Villoresi brothers in their 508CS Balilla Sport also finishing 14th overall. The Targa Florio took place soon after the Mille Miglia, with Francesco Toia winning the up to 1100cc class in his Fiat 508 Coppa d'Oro, but the fastest lap was set by Albino

A 508 Coppa d'Oro model waiting to start at a hillclimb in Lewes in 1938. (Courtesy FF)

Ferrara who also drove a 508 Coppa d'Oro. The result was no great surprise, as of the six starters in the up to 1100cc class, only one was not a Fiat, and it failed to finish; the overall winner being Antonio Brivo in an Alfa Romeo. It is interesting to note that the overall winner's average speed for the race was 49.2mph, whilst that of Toia in his little Fiat was 40.5mph and Ferrara's fastest lap was 41.2mph.

The third and final Czechoslovak 1000-mile race took place during June and saw 508s take first, third, fifth and sixth places in the up to 1100cc class; the first in class also finished in tenth place overall and was driven by Ruggerio Minio and Vittore Gollavo. The precise reason for 1935 being the last race will probably never be known, but there appear to be two principal factors. Firstly, there had been a number of accidents in all three races, some involving fatalities and serious injuries. Secondly, the 1000-mile race was conceived as a way of promoting the Czechoslovak motor industry and the fact that in the 1935 event, out of five classes, four were won by foreign competitors didn't help. As a result Czech car manufacturers were unwilling to enter an event that was likely to promote competitors' products rather than their own.

A significant person who made an impact in 1935 was Amédée Gordini, who would

FIAT IN MOTORSPORT SINCE 1899

Above: In the paddock at the Prescott hillclimb meeting.

Opposite, top: A 508 exiting the hairpin at a Mallory Park VSCC meeting.

Below: A 508 Sport at the Loton Park hillclimb.

1930s–1940s: A Quieter Period

Felice Nazzaro in a 508 Sport.

become famous after the Second World War, in particular for his Formula 1 and Formula 2 Grand Prix cars, although he also produced racing sports cars. Amédée Gordini was born in Bazzano, Italy and, prior to the First World War, worked as a mechanic for Alfieri Maserati. Following the war, in which he served in the Italian Army, he moved to France and eventually settled in Paris. There he commenced his career as a racing driver using specially tuned Fiat Balillas. In conjunction with Henri Pigozzi, who was the French representative for Fiat, in 1934 Gordini started building Fiats under Pigozzi's Simca organisation. Gordini joined Simca and soon became head of its motor racing department. His talent for improving performance earned him the nickname of 'the sorcerer.' His improvements to the Balillas included reducing the weight, and numerous engine modifications to the extent that it was said 'the only remaining Fiat components were the bore and stroke.' Gordini Fiats scored class wins in the Circuit d'Orleans, the Bol d'Or and the Marne Grand Prix, usually driven by

Left: A Walter 'Junior' in the 1933 Czech 1000-mile trial. Right: Walters lining up before the start of the 1934 Czech 1000-mile trial.

Gordini himself. In the County Down Trophy Race in Northern Ireland, which had been granted international status that year, Ffrench-Davis finished second in his Fiat Balilla. Also in Northern Ireland, three Fiat Balillas were entered in the Ards TT race, but none finished due to insufficient laps completed, engine trouble or lack of fuel.

Another personality who appeared in 1935 was Piero Dusio, later to become famous due to his founding of the firm Cisitalia, immediately after the end of the Second World War. In that year's Mille Miglia he entered a berlinetta aerodynamica, which had a very streamlined nose and a supercharged engine: however, he failed to complete the course.

Future Grand Prix driver Luigi Villoresi took a class victory in the Grossglockner hillclimb and in the Targa Abruzzo; in addition to winning their class, Fiats also finished fourth and fifth overall. Despite combining the 1100cc and 1500cc classes in the Lorraine Grand Prix, the Fiats, led by Gordini, finished first, second and third. European hillclimb victories included

1500 Viotti-bodied berlinettas at the 1937 Mille Miglia. (Courtesy FCA)

Eymountiers, Stelvio, Feldberg, Mount Gugger and Harmashatar.

1936 started well for Fiat with Kozma and Martinek finishing 11th overall in the Monte Carlo Rally, and the Mille Miglia saw Biagini and Periccioli win their class in a 508CS Balilla. In England, Westwood and Tett received first class awards in the RAC Rally, and Tett then won the Blackpool Rally outright. At Brooklands, the Light Car Club's relay race saw one of the three Fiat teams that were taking part finish fourth. This team was all female, and they beat the other male dominated teams.

Stothert won a first-class award in his Balilla at the Torquay rally in July. The 1936 TT races were held on the Ards circuit for the last time and attracted four Fiat 508S Balillas. Of the four, two failed to finish, one was not classified, but the remaining one, driven by Billie Sullivan, won his class despite finishing in 13th place out of just 15 finishers.

Gordini continued to score victories in his Simca/Fiat; his wins included the Bol d'Or and a class win in the 24-hour race at Spa in Belgium. The Eifelrennen in Germany resulted in a one, two, three, four finish in class, led by Brendel.

This year's Targa Florio was a somewhat sad affair with only 11 entries. The race was over two laps of the Madonie circuit, and saw a clean sweep by Lancia. The best placed Fiat was in fifth position, closely followed by another. There is some confusion as to which model of Fiat took part; in some accounts they are recorded as Balillas and in others as 1500s. However, what is not in dispute is the fact that Romano Malaguti finished fifth overall out of nine finishers. The two retirements were both Fiats. The 1500 had been introduced at the 1935 Milan Motor Show and was powered by a six-cylinder, overhead valve 1493cc engine that produced 45bhp. It was, at the time, considered to be an outstanding example of modern aerodynamic design. Open versions were manufactured as well as traditional saloons and over its 13 year life more than 42,000 were produced. It was, however, a model hardly ever seen in competition.

At the 1937 Monte Carlo Rally, Luigi Villoresi had won the light car class in a 1500, finishing in 13th place overall. The Mille Miglia saw the now usual Fiat class wins, with Minio and Castagnaro finishing 12th overall and taking the 1500cc honours in their 1500 Spider, and Colini and Prosperi finishing 24th overall and winning their class in their 508CS Balilla Sport. The class winning 1500 was one of two Viotti-bodied specials, the second one, driven by Vittorio Mussolini, son of the 'Duce,' failed to finish. An interesting aside is the entry of Morettini of a 508 Sport that had been modified by him. Sadly it failed to complete the race, but today the car still exists and took part in the 2011 Mille Miglia; on this occasion it finished the event in 13th place!

Viotti was a coachbuilder and designer who

Above: A 1936 Morettini Fiat 508S at the 2011 Mille Miglia.

Left: Rear view of the Morettini.

designed a number of elegant vehicles, not just for Fiat, but also Lancia and Isotta Fraschini. His Fiat 1500 design was a striking, aerodynamic two-door coupé with very flowing bodywork. Further successes were achieved by Fiats at the Littorio Races held at Rome Airport, the Susa-Moncenisio hillclimb, and the Bol d'Or. In the Targa Abruzzo, Fiats finished first in three classes, with Ovidio Capelli finishing first in class and third overall in his 1500 Zagato, his average speed being 61.50mph. His car was entered by Scuderia Ambrosiana. 'Gordini' Balillas finished sixth and seventh at the Coupe de la Commission Sportive at Montlhéry. The Bol d'Or also saw a Fiat class win, as did the 'Gordini' Balillas at Le Mans; in the Prince Rainier Cup at Monaco, a 'Gordini' Balilla was the only light car in the race, but nevertheless finished fifth behind much larger cars.

In addition to the usual class wins there was another Fiat model that started to appear in the results: the Fiat 500. This new model had first appeared in April 1936 as La Topolino ('Mickey Mouse'), despite being designated the 500 it had a 569cc four-cylinder side-valve engine and could only hold two people. Designed by a new team, comprising Dante Giacosa and Professor Antonio Fessia, it was a groundbreaking new design. It was second only to the English Austin Seven as a true utility vehicle available to anyone. Over a remarkable lifetime of 19 years, more than 500,000 were to emerge from Turin alone, apart from those built elsewhere. After the Second World War, its chassis and suspension were used as the basis for 500cc Formula 3 racing cars.

Professor Fessia was born in Turin in 1901, and joined Fiat in 1925. Dante Giacosa was born in Rome in 1905, joining Fiat in 1928. They both obtained engineering degrees at Turin's Polytechnic, and were employed in Fiat's aero engine division at the same time. Giacosa once recalled, "My job was to design a small car that would be comfortable, functional and safe at the lowest possible production cost. Once weight calculations were complete for all assemblies comprising the chassis my conclusion was that it would be possible to avoid exceeding a total weight of 250kg. A weight of 180-200kg had been forecast for the bodywork. With a total weight of 450kg it would then be possible to sell the car at a price of about 12 lire per kilo as against 17 lire for the three-speed Balilla." Giacosa again "I assigned the engine design to Virgilio Borsattino ... it was the simplest version possible of a four-cylinder, water cooled engine; no water pumps, no petrol pump, a rudimentary oil pump, no timing regulation, and a crankshaft with only two main bearings. A more economical construction than this was impossible."

The model soon attracted the attention of the 'tuners' such as Stanguellini, Gordini and Siata, with some offering overhead-valve conversions. The Topolino soon started to record class victories, for example in the Mille Miglia, 500s scored class wins in both the 750cc sporting and touring classes. The fastest finisher, driven by Dusio, averaged nearly 50mph for the 1000-mile race. In the Paris to Nice Rally, Hervé Coatalen won the 750cc class; he was the son of the famous designer, Louis. In the 24-hour race at Le Mans that year, Viale and Alin drove their 500 into 17th and last place having averaged a very creditable 52.09mph for the race.

Due to the increasing Mercedes-Benz and Auto Union teams' dominance in Grand Prix racing, from 1937 until the Second World War it was decided to run the Targa Florio as a voiturette race, ie for single seat racing cars not exceeding 1500cc. Whilst this was successful in keeping the German teams away, it did result in domination by Maserati who won all the remaining races that took place prewar, including the 1940 event that took place before Italy entered the war. As a consequence no Fiats took part in the Targa Florio during this period. This year saw the birth of Squadra Stanguellini formed by Vittorio

A 500 Topolino on display at the Centro Historico.

Stanguellini, who had established an excellent reputation as a tuner of Fiat cars.

During 1938, however, several changes were taking place. Firstly Fiat was developing the Savio–bodied 508CMM coupé, which now had a 1089cc engine. The 508C had been introduced in 1937 as the Balilla 1100; it had a 1089cc overhead valve engine that produced 32bhp, and had a four-speed gearbox with synchromesh on third and fourth gears. Its styling reflected the revised design introduced on the 1935 1500, and it was an immediate success, with over 250,000 being manufactured between 1937 and 1939. The 'Mille Miglia' version was introduced in 1938, with drophead editions being available in addition to normal saloons. The 508C was the first of the world-famous 'millecento' series, a name that was to remain in the company's catalogue for many years. The Mille Miglia version, or 508CMM, had an aerodynamic body built by Savio. Due to its low drag body, the 508CMM could produce an astonishing performance for an 1100cc car; 95mph was achievable in top gear. Carrozzeria Savio was established in 1919 by two brothers, Antonio and Giuseppe Savio, who had finished their apprenticeship at the Alessio coachworks in Turin. Initially, they secured a contract with Itala which ultimately led to work with Fiat, for whom they enjoyed a long-term relationship. The firm still exists today and, in 1995, took over the failing Boneschi carrozzeria; its main work currently is bodywork for trucks, buses and other commercial vehicles.

Other developments to the 1089cc 508C model were also being undertaken by Gordini and an English tuner called Tuson. In the Monte Carlo Rally a Dr Manicatide, having started from Bucharest, finish 26th overall and second in class, it is not recorded which model he drove, although in the 1939 event he finished 28th overall and was described as driving a Fiat 1500 that he may have used the year before. Gordini won the Paris to Nice outright in one of his Simca specials, as he did in the Bol d'Or.

The Mille Miglia results again featured Fiats in a class win, with Piero Taruffi and Francesco Carena finishing first in class in their 1100 MM coupé bodied by Savio. Both a 1500 Spider Zagato and a 508CS Balilla Sport finished second in their respective classes. Sadly, the race experienced a number of accidents resulting in 10 fatalities and 23 injuries; for this reason the 1939 race was cancelled.

Gordini entered a team of his Simca-Fiats for that year's Le Mans 24-hour race, the Simca-Fiat Balillas and a single Simca-Huit, which had an 1100cc engine, and all but one retired; the remaining car finished ninth overall and second in class. However, Gordini had also entered two Simca-Cinqs that were Fiat 500s built under licence; these completed the whole race and finished 14th and 15th overall, winning their class and the all-important Index of Performance.

The 1939 Monte Carlo Rally results show that, having started from Athens, Gordini and Scaron took 13th place overall. Allegedly organised to replace the cancelled Mille Miglia, the 1000-mile Tobruk to Tripoli marathon took place during March, and Fiats dominated both the 1100cc and 750cc classes. Interestingly, the overall winning car, an Alfa Romeo 6C 2300, was driven by Benito Mussolini's chauffeur, Ercola Borato, and Consalvo Sanesi, who did most of the driving. At Le Mans in June, Gordini finished a very creditable 10th and won the Rudge-Whitworth Cup. At the Reims Grand Prix meeting held on July 9, he won the Coupe de la Commission Sportive. His final outing before war broke out was at the Grand Prix de Comminges, where, against much larger and powerful cars, he finished third overall.

Whilst Europe was steeling itself against the prospect of another war, in Britain, Anthony Heal scored several wins in his now rather ancient S61, the last of which was a mere two days before Britain went to war.

A Savio-bodied 508CMM showing low-drag design.

1930s-1940s: A Quieter Period

A 'Mille Miglia' Berlinetta at a hillclimb in 1938. (Courtesy FF)

1940 Auto Avia 815.

In Italy, which didn't enter the war until June 1940, some events still took place. The 1940 Mille Miglia took place on April 28, but was run over a much shorter course of just over 100 miles, which had to be lapped nine times and was called the 'Gran Premio delle Brescia.' Despite the tense political situation, in addition to the German BMW team, there was also an entry of two Delages (but to be driven by Italians!). Fiat was well represented in the 750 class with Siata modified versions, while the 1100cc and 1500cc classes had a number of Stanguellini versions. The German BMW team dominated the race, with the charismatic Baron Huschke von Hanstein and Walter Baumer leading from the start; they were never seriously challenged by the eventual second place Alfa Romeo driven by Giuseppe Farina and Paride Mambelli. In terms of Fiat, it was victorious in both the 750cc and 1100cc classes, but had to be satisfied with second in the 1500cc class. An interesting entry was two Auto Avia 815s entered by Enzo Ferrari. In 1938 Enzo Ferrari had left Alfa Romeo where he had been running its racing division under 'Scuderia Ferrari.' His settlement with Alfa Romeo had forbidden him from restarting 'Scuderia Ferrari' for four years, so he established 'Auto Avio Construzioni' in Modena to manufacture aircraft parts. However, during late 1939 he was approached with a request to build two racing cars for the 1940 Mille Miglia. As his settlement with Alfa Romeo forbade him to use his name on the cars, he called them the Auto Avia 815s (the 8 representing the number of cylinders and 15 the engine size). It has been reported on many occasions that the engine was based upon two Fiat 508 engines placed in line and utilised many Fiat components. However, eminent Fiat historian, the late Michael Sedgwick, claimed that while chassis frames, suspensions, gearboxes, differentials, steering boxes and cylinder heads were genuine Fiat components, the blocks had been cast in Modena by Calzoni and the single Marelli distributor replaced the dual arrangement used by Fiat. The open bodies were designed by Carrozzeria Touring. Despite both cars leading their class at various stages of the race, both subsequently retired with engine problems; one of the cars was driven by future World Champion Alberto Ascari.

The Targa Florio was run on May 23, but was still run under voiturette rules, so Fiats weren't involved.

Naturally, the Second World War resulted in the cessation of European motor racing until the conflict ended in 1945. France was very quick off the mark and organised a race meeting in the Bois de Boulogne on 9th September 1945. In 1946, the ninth French Alpine Rally took place and, unsurprisingly, all 37 starters used prewar cars. The 1100cc class was won by future Grand Prix driver, Robert Manzon, who was driving a Fiat-based Simca-Huit. In the 750cc class, a Simca-Cinq take first place; Simca also won the Team Prize. The following year's event saw a repeat of the 1946 results, albeit with different drivers; this also included the Team Prize. In September the Grand Prix of Turin took place in the city's Valentino Park, the Grand Prix was accompanied by a voiturette race. This latter race was won by a newcomer having its first race. This 'newcomer' was a Cisitalia driven by its founder Piero Dusio. Cisitalia Automobile SpA was founded by Piero Dusio immediately after the Second World War. Dusio was a wealthy sportsman, and was assisted by racing driver Piero Taruffi and engineer Giovanni Savonuzzi. Based upon a tuned Balilla engine, the single seat D46 first appeared in 1946, initially intended as an inexpensive racer to compete in its own special races, it was of course eligible for voiturette events. The D46 made an instant impact, sometimes against much more powerful competitors. In fact, at the aforementioned event at Valentino Park in Turin, Dusio won driving one of his new cars and another finished in third place.

In October, a Cisitalia driven by de Sauge finished fourth at the Penya Rhin Grand Prix held on the Pedralbes circuit near Barcelona, against Formula 1 competition. At the Circuit des Ramparts held at Angoulême, in France, D46s driven by Michelet and Loyer finished in second and third places respectively. Also in France, Simca-Gordinis scored several wins. As in prewar days, Amedée Gordini continued to race the Simca-Gordinis that were still using a Fiat-based engine, although continued development meant that not much of the original remained. Their light weight and manoeuvrability, similar to the Cisitalia, offset the lack of power on tortuous circuits and resulted in many wins. In France at least six wins were recorded in events such as the Coupe de la Méditeranée and the Grand Prix de Bourgogne.

The prewar 508CMM was revamped during 1947, retaining its Savio body, but with a revised waterfall-style grille, and, due to a revised tail, was ten inches shorter, but now had a proper rear window! Due to the fitting of two downdraught Weber carburettors there was an increase in power and a slight increase in compression ratio, giving a power output of 51bhp at 5200rpm. Weight was reduced by the adoption of lightweight alloy for the bodies, and the seats were staggered to allow more elbow room in the narrow cabin. Only 401 of these amazing little cars were produced between 1947 and 1950. The revised car was now designated the 1100S and immediately became highly successful in competition. Its first appearance as a prototype was at the 1947 Sassi to Superga hillclimb driven by the factory test driver, Carlo Salamano.

1947 also saw the first postwar Mille Miglia take place. Due to the ravages of war-torn Italy, a revised route was devised avoiding the worst damaged sections of the country, but the start and finish remained in Brescia. The entry list was a diverse mixture of the old and new, with some new names to add to the old established makes. An astonishing 245 entries were received, although 90 failed to start. The fact that all entrants were provided with a new set of Pirelli tyres and a full tank of petrol, both free of charge may have had some impact on the number of entries received! Building on the success of the D46, Cisitalia produced a two-seat sports racer known as the 202 (this is described in greater detail in Chapter 6). The race turned into an epic struggle between the smaller engine cars and the more powerful Alfa Romeos. Initially the race was led by one of the new Fiat 1100S driven by Bassi, but at Rome Nuvolari and Carena in the tiny Cisitalia 202 were in the lead, hotly pursued by Biondetti and Romano in their Alfa Romeo 8C 2900B Berlinetta. At Florence the positions remained the same, however from then onwards the weather deteriorated badly, and, as a consequence, Nuvolari in the open Cisitalia was at a distinct disadvantage compared to Biondetti who had the benefit of being in a closed coupé. Unfortunately conditions were so atrocious that at one point Nuvolari's car was swamped by water and the electrics were flooded, resulting in the engine stalling; it took Nuvolari and Carena some 15 minutes to re-start the engine. As a consequence, despite his best efforts, Nuvolari had to give best to the Alfa Romeo and finished in second place after 16 hours of racing.

The new Fiat 1100S models, despite the disappointment of Bassi's slip down the placings, performed admirably. Three of the cars, led by Capelli, finished in fifth, sixth and seventh places. The early leader, Bassi eventually finished in 53rd place overall and 20th and last in class, presumably having experienced some difficulties at some stage. Interestingly, the ubiquitous Fiat 500s again featured in the results with Capelli winning his class and finishing in 45th place overall, having taken just over 24 hours to complete the race.

Elsewhere, Cisitalia continued to do well. In a minor race at Hockenheim in May, former Auto-Union driver, Hans Stuck, driving a D46 finished in first place. At the Coup Robert Benoist in early June Raymond Sommer,

Cisitalia D46.

1930s-1940s: A Quieter Period

1100S on display in Centro Historico.

Robert Manzon and Harry Schell finished second, third and fourth. In the same month in Italy, Piero Taruffi scored wins at the Circuito di Vercelli and Circuito di Caracalla. Still in Italy, Felice Bonetto came first in the Circuito di Vigerano, with other D46s finishing third, fourth and fifth. At the Circuit des Ramparts at Angoulême in France, Robert Manzon finished second ahead of Roger Loyer, both in their D46s. Loyer took part in the Coupe de Paris in July and came home third, whilst in the Coupe des Petite Cylindres at Reims the highest placed D46 was driven by Robert Manzon into fourth place, followed by Schell. Back in Italy the Gran Premio Luigi Arcangeli, the Circuito del Montenero and the Circuito del Lido di Venezia all saw D46 Cisitalias come first. Finally, in the race named in his honour, the legendary Tazio Nuvolari finished second at Mantua.

As in 1946, the Simca-Gordinis continued to be successful at appropriate circuits. These

Side view showing streamlined profile. (Courtesy GR)

FIAT IN MOTORSPORT SINCE 1899

Spotted in Rome in 1951 – an 1100S. (Courtesy FF)

1100S at the 2011 Mille Miglia.

Another 1100S at the 2011 Mille Miglia.

successes also included sports cars, which triumphed at the Bol c'Or. In terms of the single-seater cars, in June, Jean-Pierre Wimille won the Coupe de Robert Benoist (named after the prewar French racing driver killed by the Nazis during the Second World War). In July he also won the Coupe de Paris, and in September finished third to B Bira in the Coupe de Lyon (Bira was also driving a Gordini). Bira had several successes in his Gordini, he won the Coupe de Petite Cylindres in July, the Manx Cup in August and the Prix de Leman in October. He also finished second in the Coupe de Lyon followed by Wimille.

The Tarca Florio resumed in 1948 after a seven year break due to the Second World War and attracted a huge entry of almost 100 cars. To avoid a similar incident as happened in last year's Mille Miglia, Cisitalia entered two closed coupés to be driven by Taruffi/Rabbia and Macchieraldo/Savio. The entry list also included numerous Fiat models. In the race itself, amazingly, despite a significant power disadvantage compared to some of the other competitors, Taruffi, in his Cisitalia Coupé, led for much of the 670-mile race, only to be beaten into second place by Biondetti who

Brivio and Maggi in their 1100S racing to 13th place in the 1947 Mille Miglia. (Courtesy NMM)

was driving a much more powerful Ferrari 166; Taruffi was only 16 minutes behind the winner at the end. His Cisitalia team-mate finished third. It was a good day for the Fiat entries with class wins for 1100s and 500s.

Four weeks later, the 15th Mille Miglia took place, and turned out to be a remarkable race for several reasons. Firstly, the legendary Tazio Nuvolari, who was now 55 years of age and suffering bad health, had not expected to race, but when the wealthy Lithuanian gentleman, Igor Troubetskoy, withdrew from his Ferrari team drive, Enzo Ferrari immediately offered it to Nuvolari who accepted enthusiastically. During the race, Nuvolari, in the Ferrari 166 open sports, was leading at Rome despite a damaged car, and by Bologna he had built up a 29-minute lead over the second-placed Ferrari 166 Coupé driven by Biondetti and Navone. However, before reaching Brescia, his Ferrari suffered a suspension failure, leaving Biondetti to take his third Mille Miglia victory, which, in itself, was a magnificent achievement.

The second notable feature was the performance of the Fiat 1100S cars that actually finished second and third – a remarkable feat considering the much more powerful

Cisitalia 202 Coupé at the 2011 Mille Miglia

opponents that finished behind them. The second-placed Fiat was driven by Comirato. Fiorio drove his Fiat Siata 500 'Pescara' into first in class, having finished in 37th place overall, and Capelli drove his 1100 into a first in class, having finished in 45th place in the overall results. The Cisitalias once again put in excellent performances, particularly the one driven by Taruffi and Rabbia, which, unfortunately, had to retire before reaching Rome. However, a Cisitalia 202 Berlinetta finished in fifth place overall.

The 1949 Targa Florio took place on March 20, and whilst the race was dominated by the more powerful Ferraris and Alfa Romeos, Fiats managed to secure no fewer than four class wins! The highest placed Fiat was a 1100 Sport driven by Emanuele and Giovanni de Maria, who finished sixth overall and first in the 1100 class. Other class wins were attained by 1100B, 500B and 750 Sport models. The 1100 Fiat that took victory in that class was driven by Lucien De Sanctis, who, in the late1950s, manufactured and drove Formula Junior cars under his own name.

The Mille Miglia took place on April 24, and had the customary 'swarm' of Fiats competing. The course now returned to its original prewar route and attracted a record 303 starters, some 182 of which actually completed the course. The race turned out to be a duel between the three works Ferraris, ending in a victory for Biondetti and Salani, with Bonetto and Taruffi both retiring in the other team Ferraris. What an achievement for Biondetti: four Mille Miglia victories, the last three consecutive! Not only did the 50-year-old Biondetti win four Mille Miglias, he also won two Targa Florios (1948 and 1949), but was less successful in single seat racing. In fourth place overall, and first in the 1100cc class, came Auricchio and Bozzini in their 1100S Berlinetta. Second and third in this class were a Cisitalia and another 1100S Berlinetta. In the 24 hours of Le Mans, a Simca Cinq finished 14th overall and 3rd in class.

At the 1949 Geneva Motor Show Fiat, announced that an updated 1100S coupé was being introduced. The new model, known as the 1100ES, was, in a first for Fiat, to be fitted with a Pininfarina-styled body. This was an important step for Pininfarina as it represented the start of the company moving from a producer of one-off special bodies for customers to a much larger manufacturer. The modifications to the car included a modern close-coupled style that could now accommodate four people. The body style closely resembled that of the

FIAT IN MOTORSPORT SINCE 1899

Nuvolari's Ferrari 166 as it is today.

Cisitalia 202 coupé, which is unsurprising as that 1947 design was also by Pininfarina and could also be seen in the 1950 Lancia Aurelia GT coupé.

This era saw the start of the production of many Fiat based specials or 'etcerinis' as they are otherwise known; these are covered in some detail in Chapter 6.

1950 1100ES with body by Pininfarina.

CHAPTER FIVE
The 1950s and a New Venture

The 1952 Geneva Motor Show took place during March, and one of the new models that took everyone by surprise was a Fiat sports coupé known as the 8V or Otto Vu. Designer Dante Giacose and stylist Fabio Luigi Rapi had come up with an entirely new design utilising a V8 engine, which was a first for Fiat and one that it has never repeated since. The body was futuristically styled by Rapi and featured a long bonnet with a sharply inclined windscreen, while the rear section was rounded. It was a two-seater with competition clearly in mind, as could seen from the seating arrangement that had the passenger seat set several inches back from the driver's seat, thus allowing the driver plenty of 'arm room' in the confined cockpit, similar to the 1100S. The original brief for the engine stipulated that it should be a narrow angle 'V' configuration with a capacity of 1995cc. This requirement was made to ensure the engine would fit in an existing engine bay, and, as a consequence, a 70-degree layout was adopted. In its standard form, with twin downdraught double-choke Weber carburettors, the 72 x 61.3mm engine produced some 105bhp, and gave the car a top speed of 120mph (or thereabouts, depending which road test is adopted). It had all round independent suspension and 11.4in drum brakes front and back.

Fiat eventually implemented some alterations to the original design; this became the second series. Sadly, it had a very short life of just two years, and only 114 were manufactured. It is believed that Fiat considered the effort required to build these exceptional cars and the attendant high price could not be justified, and that it should concentrate its efforts on providing low cost cars that would attract the most customers. Subsequently some chassis were supplied to various carrozeria such as Vignale, Pininfarina, Ghia and Zagato, which produced their own versions.

First series 8V on the Fiat test track. (Courtesy GR)

As it was intended for competition, the V8 did achieve some success. Its first victory came in the 1952 Stella Alpine Rally when a Zagato-bodied 8V driven by Ovidio Capelli won outright, in addition, during that year, he also took class wins at Rocca di Papa, the Pescara 12 Hours, the Coppa Internazionale di Monza and the Giro dell'Umbria.

In that year's Mille Miglia, an 8V driven by Auricchio and Bozzini finished 15th and 4th in class. At the same event in 1953, Cortese and Feroldi finished 14th and 4th in class. 1954 saw Elio Zagato win the 3 Hours of Bari, and 9th place overall and 2nd in class was achieved by the Leto di Priolo brothers in that year's Mille Miglia, another driven by the Poillucci brothers finished 18th. Elio Zagato, who was the son of Ugo Zagato, founder of Carrozeria Zagato, also won that year's Coppa Intereuropa at Monza.

The 1954 2-litre GT Championship of Italy

First series 8V rear view. (Courtesy GR)

was another noteworthy achievement. Despite only being in production for just over two years, 8Vs continued to make an impact for several more years. 1955 witnessed the famous Stirling Moss and Denis Jenkinson's record-breaking victory in the Mille Miglia, driving a Mercedes-Benz 300SLR, averaging an astonishing 97.95mph for the 1000 miles, a record that was never to be beaten. In the same race, Castelbarco and Savoretti drove their 8V Zagato into 13th place and 4th in class. In the Targa Florio, Elio Zagato and Capelli finished in 11th place and 1st in class, behind them another 8V Zagato finished 13th and 2nd in class.

1956 results saw 8Vs take class wins in both the Mille Miglia and Targa Florio races, they finished 14th overall in the former and 11th in the latter. In 1957, Ludovico Sarfiotti made

Second series 8V – note slight changes to the front. (Courtesy GR)

Second series 8V front view. (Courtesy GR))

Centro Storico's second series 8V.

8V by Pininfarina. (Courtesy GR)

fastest time of the day in the Aosta-St Bernard hillclimb and, whilst only finishing in 34th place in the Mille Miglia, Nobile and Cagnana were 1st in class in their 8V Zagato. In 1958 one finished 13th in the Targa Florio and 1st in class. So ended the racing career of this exciting car; the late Michael Sedgwick once described the 8V as "technicians thinking aloud."

An interesting development of the 8V was by Siata, who utilised the engine, transmission and suspension from the original model to produce a sports car, the Siata 208, with Siata's own designed space frame chassis and bodywork. Further tuning of the engine eventually increased the power output to 126bhp at 6000rpm. The 208 remained in production until 1955, outliving Fiat's own 8V by over a year; total production was 56 (some sources quote 53), of which 18 were coupés and the remainder roadsters/spiders.

Apart from the 8V, the 1950s continued to see the Fiat name in race results, whether as actual Fiat models or as the increasing number of Fiat engined specials, or 'etceterinis' as they are sometimes called. The races involved were usually endurance events, either for pure sports racing cars or grand touring (GT) models; this situation applied until the introduction of Formula Junior in 1958, covered in Chapter 7.

The 1950 Targa Florio saw a swathe of class wins for Fiat-based specials. A Fiat Ermini 1100 Sport was 4th overall, a Giannini 750S was 23rd, a Fiat 1100E was 33rd and a Fiat 500 was 52nd, all finishing first in their respective classes. In the Mille Miglia, out of 204 finishers, Fiats scored wins in the 1100 (Touring) and 750 classes. The

8V by Ghia. (Courtesy GR)

8V by Zagato at the 2011 Mille Miglia.

highest placed Fiat was an 1100E that finished 11th overall and 2nd in that category. A single Fiat 1500 was entered for Brault and Paimpol in the Le Mans 24 hour race, but retired after 75 laps with gearbox problems; this was the last time that a 'pure' Fiat took part in this race as future entries were from specialist makes.

Two more class wins came in the 1951 Targa Florio when an Abarth Cisitalia finished 4th overall and a 750 Siata finished 7th overall and last. There had been a smaller than usual entry of just 25 cars, and only 7 were classed as finishers. That year's Mille Miglia saw Fiats and Fiat-based specials attain four class wins. An event that straddled both 1951 and 1952 was the Algiers to Cape Town and back 'raid' that started on November 25 and finished on January 14. Two Fiat 'Campagnola' 4x4 cross-country vehicles were entered, and both completed the 9300 mile route. The winning Fiat set a new record for crossing the Sahara Desert with a vehicle and trailer in six and a half days. The 'Campagnola' was a 1900cc four-wheel-drive off-road vehicle designed for military use.

1952 international motorsport season commenced with the 22nd running of the Monte Carlo Rally. The rally was run under extremely difficult weather conditions and

Hair and Veronelli on the start ramp for the 1952 Mille Miglia – they didn't finish. (Courtesy FCA)

the husband and wife team of Dr M and Mme Angelvin brought their Simca Huit Sport into third place. The Targa Florio of 1952 saw class wins by an Ermini and a Stanguellini 750. The 8V's results have already been itemised earlier in this chapter, but in that year's Mille Miglia a Siata 208S, driven by Rol and Munaron finished 11th overall and 3rd in class. In other categories Fiats notched up three more class wins, including a 1400 that appeared in the results for the first time.

Launched at the 1950 Geneva Motor Show, the new 1400 replaced the existing 1100 and 1500 models, although the 1100S was revamped and continued in production for some years. The 1400 was Fiat's first production car to have a monocoque body, and had clear American influences in its overall design. The 1953 Mille Miglia results only included one class win: despite finishing 78th, a Fiat 1100 was first in class. The 1100 also proved to be a successful rally car. In 1953 German rally driver Helmut Polensky won that year's European Touring Challenge in an 1100 by winning the 3rd International Freiburg to Travemünde Rally, and finishing second in the Viking Rally in Norway. In both events a Fiat 1100 also finished in fourth place. At the 1953 Geneva Motor Show a revamped 1100 was launched, now known as the 1100-103. Basically it was an entirely new design, even the engine, although superficially similar to the previous 1089cc unit, was new. Then, at that year's Paris Motor Show, the 103 TV was announced; 'TV' stood for 'Turismo Veloce' and was a higher performance version.

1954 results included three class wins in the Targa Florio (1100 Sports and Touring and 750 Sport) and one in the 1100 Touring class at the Mille Miglia. The following year's results saw two more class wins in the Mille Miglia. In the Targa Florio of 1956 a Giaur Giannini 750 scored a class win, whilst in that year's Mille Miglia, Ludovico Scarfiotti finished in 57th place, but first in class, in a Fiat 1100/103 TV. Similar models also took second and third in that class. Domenico Ogna took his tiny Fiat-Abarth 750 to first place in the production 750 Grand Touring class.

In rallying there were more successes. In the Tulip Rally in Holland, Martens finished fifth overall, but first in class. Samsing was third in the Viking Rally, with another 1100 in fifth place, and in the Polish Rally, Witkowski finished second.

In 1956, apart from the 8V's results listed earlier, Ludivico Scarfiotti won his class in the Mille Miglia driving an 1100/103. In the Targa Florio, Piccolo, driving a Giaur Giannini 750 Sport, won his class and finished 16th overall. In the tough East African Coronation Safari Rally, 1100s finished second and fourth. This event, which was renamed the East African Safari Rally in 1960 and then the Safari Rally in 1974, traversed countries that were then named as Kenya, Uganda and Tanganyika.

The 1957 Monte Carlo Rally was cancelled because of the Suez crisis of late 1956. The disastrous Mille Miglia of 1957, which was the last one held due to the tragic deaths of Alfonse de Portago, his co-driver Ed Nelson and ten spectators (including five children) that led to it being banned, saw three more class wins for Fiat. In 63rd place overall, but first in class, was a Fiat-Abarth 750 Zagato driven by Alfonso Thiele, while Mandrini and Bertassi drove their 1100/103 into 91st place, but first in class, and Dino Faggi finished in 108th place overall, but again first in class. Although the Mille Miglia road race has never taken place again since 1957, for several years now a Mille Miglia `retrospective` has been run, entries for which are restricted to makes and models of cars that took place in the original race.

That year's Targa Florio took place in November instead of May, due to the ban on road races following the tragic Mille Miglia. It was run as a regularity contest rather than a race and was over five laps instead of ten. Victory went to Fabio Colonna in a Fiat 600. The relatively unknown Colonna beat two Lancia Appias, the first of which was driven by the well known Piero Taruffi, who earlier in the year had won the Mille Miglia in a Ferrari. In the East African Safari Rally, an 1100 driven by Armstrong and Temple-Boreham won its class, which was then based upon list price. This year's Le Mans 24-hour race saw the first Fiat-based entry since 1950. Two Stanguellini 'Bialbero' cars, one an 1100 and the other a 750 were entered, but both failed to finish.

For the reasons outlined above, there was no Mille Miglia in 1958. Ferrari dominated the Targa Florio, filling three out of the first four places. However, in 11th place overall, but first in class, was the Fiat Raor Sport driven by di Silvo and Minneci.

1958 was also a milestone year for Fiat in that, as referred to earlier, a new category of

Elio Zagato winning the 1954 Coppa Intereuropa at Monza. (Courtesy FCA)

An 8V at a control/checkpoint at an event in France. (Courtesy NMM)

single-seat racing was introduced, Formula Junior, which initially relied heavily on Fiat-based cars. This is explored in detail in Chapter 7. At Le Mans, three Stanguellinis were entered and one, a Stanguellini 750 Sport driven by Sigrand and Révillon, finished 19th overall and seventh in class; the other two failed to finish.

In 1958 an unusual event took place. In the aftermath of the 1957 Suez crisis, a rally for cars with engines under 500cc was organised. The Liège-Brescia-Liège rally was only held once, and was a clear demonstration of the Fiat 500's endurance capability. Seven 500s started and all seven finished, filling the first five places.

In the 1959 Le Mans 24-hour race there were only 13 finishers and in 13th place was the Stanguellini 750 Sport driven by Delageneste and Guirad, but was not classified due to their failure to complete the required 70% of the winner's distance. The winner's race distance was 323 laps and the Stanguellini managed only 220 by the end of the race which represents 68%. There had been three Stanguellinis entered, but two retired for a variety of reasons. A Fiat-Abarth 750 Zagato driven by Carini and Prinoth finished in 14th place overall, and first in the GT750 class. The 1959 Targa Florio was dominated by Porsche, which swept to an overwhelming finish after a furious battle with the works Ferraris. Led by Barth and Seidel, Porsches filled the top four places; however, in 17th place overall and first in class was the Fiat-Abarth 750 Zagato driven by Carini and Prinoth.

Chapter Six
Fiat-based Specials

Fiat-based specials are more commonly called 'etceterini,' the meaning of which can be described as 'a generic term that covers a group of Italian manufacturers of small-engined sports and racing cars.' In terms of racing they appeared mostly in Italy and the USA, until the introduction of Formula Junior when the series was eventually adopted at international level. This chapter concentrates on the sports/endurance specials, while the Formula Junior constructors feature in the next chapter. There will inevitably be some duplication due to some constructors' involvement in both sectors. Also, it has to be stated that it has not been possible to detail every small constructor due to the significant numbers involved. Constructors are listed in alphabetical order, not related to success in competition or numbers made.

As mentioned in the foreword, readers may be surprised to see constructors such as Cisitala, Siata and Gordini included. These highly specialised constructors made a significant contribution to Fiat's motor sporting achievements by utilising many parts, especially engines, from production models.

Bandini
Having taken part in the 1940 Mille Miglia driving a Fiat Balilla, as soon as the Second World War ended, Ilario Bandini resumed his racing career, but in a car of his own design and bearing his own name. Utilising a modified Fiat 1100 engine, this lightweight sports car had an aluminium body of traditional style, incorporating cycle wings. These continued to be produced until 1950 when Bandini introduced what was possibly his best known model, the 750. This was a front-engined two-seater, the engine of which had double overhead camshafts and twin Weber carburettors. With the passenger seat covered and the cycle wings removed, the Bandini 750 did well in Italian Formula 3 events (in Italy engine sizes of up to 750cc were allowed in Formula 3, unlike Britain where the maximum capacity was 500cc). In 1959 he produced a Formula Junior car that became very successful. Bandini continued to manufacture open sports and coupés until 1992. The cars were very popular in the United States and won several national class championships. During the 1950s Crosley engines were used with special Bandini-designed cylinder heads. Ilario Bandini died in 1992, and in 2002 a plaza was named after him in his native city of Forli in Emilia-Romagna in recognition of his achievements. There is also a museum dedicated to him and his achievements in what used to be his workshop.

Cisitalia
Cisitalia was formed in 1946 by wealthy businessman, Piero Dusio, together with the well known racing driver, Piero Taruffi and engineer Giovanni Savonuzzi. Dusio, who had been a racing driver himself prior to the Second World War, had the ambition to build an affordable single-seat racing car based upon Fiat parts. To this end he contacted Dante Giacosa, the Fiat designer famous for his 'Topolino' design, whose extensive knowledge of Fiats was renowned. Out of this initiative emerged the Cisitalia D46, which was powered by a Fiat 1100 production engine, utilised a number of components from the Fiat 500 and 508C models, and was fitted with a pre-selector gearbox, which meant that rapid gearchanges could be achieved by depressing the clutch pedal. It had a very lightweight spaceframe chassis and the engine was tuned to give 65bhp at 5800rpm. Whilst the D46 was very competitive on the many twisty street circuits used at the time, on proper Grand Prix circuits where power and speed were critical, these cars were completely outclassed. Approximately 25 of these small, agile racing cars were constructed. Several of the D46's successes on the race track are listed in Chapter 4.

As recounted in Chapter 4 on its racing record, Cisitalia also produced a sports car, the 202, that again was based upon Fiat parts and the 1100cc engine. Battista 'Pinin' Farina was commissioned to produce a prototype and it was an immediate success; so stunning was the design that it was the first car to be displayed at the New York Museum of Modern Art. It was of spaceframe construction, and had an aerodynamic body designed by Savonuzzi. There were two versions, a GT coupé and an open two-seater. Several coachbuilders were involved in addition to Pinin Farina, these included Vignale and Stabilimenti Farina. It is still considered today to be a landmark design. Unfortunately, two factors contributed to its ultimate failure and only 170 were eventually built. Its first downfall was that it was powered by an 1100cc basic Fiat engine that failed to match the performance of the excellent roadholding characteristics it displayed; the second factor was its high cost as a result of being hand built. To illustrate this, at that time, a Jaguar XK120, which offered a much higher performance, could be purchased for half the price of the Cisitalia.

Cisitalia eventually disappeared in the early 1950s following the development of an extremely expensive Grand Prix car and founder Dusio fleeing to Argentina.

Dagrada
Angelo Dagrada was born in Milan in 1912.

Fiat-based Specials

A Bandini Formula Junior car at Oulton Park. (Courtesy PMcF)

Another view of the same car at Oulton Park. (Courtesy PMcF)

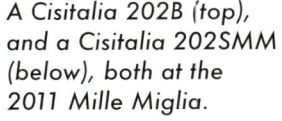

A Cisitalia 202B (top), and a Cisitalia 202SMM (below), both at the 2011 Mille Miglia.

He was initially employed at Motori Marini, but after the Second World War set up his own garage business in Milan. One day he was asked to race a Giannini 750 Sport for a customer. Dissatisfied with the performance of the Fiat 750 engine, Dagrada modified it by fitting a more reliable Siata cylinder head. Performance and reliability were improved to the extent that he was asked to build some more. He then constructed a tubular-framed special that had the Siata modified Fiat engine. It is thought that just three of these cars were built, but, nonetheless, impressive results were achieved. In 1950, Dagrada cars entered 12 races, scoring six wins and six second places. In addition to modifying the Fiat 750 engine, Dagrada also modified Fiat 1100s. Dagrada himself was involved in a serious car accident in 1950 and, after another accident two years later, he was forced to give up racing himself for a time.

In 1958, many Italian specialists were busy designing Fiat-based Formula Junior cars; Dagrada, whilst using numerous Fiat components in his design, opted to install a much modified Lancia Appia engine.

De Sanctis
The De Sanctis family, father Gino, and his son Lucio, ran a large Fiat dealership in Rome. Lucio De Sanctis designed his own car for the new Formula Junior that was introduced in 1958. His car, with a tubular space frame and coil and wishbone suspension, was very successful especially in the early years of the new formula. Initially, power was provided by a Fiat 1100cc engine, however they soon found that the Fiat engine could not compete with the likes of the Ford 105E or BMC 'A' series engines and switched to Ford engines. The cars were particularly successful in the hands of Jonathan Williams. They apparently made some sports cars, as one was entered for the 1971 Targa Florio, but failed to appear. Then the name De Sanctis disappeared from the racing scene.

Ermini
Pasquale Ermini was born in 1905 in Leccio near to Florence. During the 1920s he worked in the workshop of Emilio Materassi who ran a racing team. Tragically Materassi died in an accident at Monza in 1928, but his team carried on. It was while working with the Materassi team that Ermini met Alberto Massimino and together they developed a twin overhead camshaft cylinder head for a Fiat engine. He started his own tuning business in 1932 following the demise of the Materassi team. Following the Second World War he started constructing his own cars using his twin-cam modified Fiat 1100 engines.

The Ermini of Consolazio and Valente that failed to finish the 1952 Mille Miglia. (Courtesy FF)

An Ermini 1100 Sport at the 2011 Mille Miglia.

From 1949 until 1962, Ermini built many sports cars and they established an enviable record of racing successes, even on occasions beating much more powerful opposition such as Ferrari and Maserati.

Foglietti

Having raced Fiats and OSCAs during the 1950s, Ernesto Foglietti constructed a Formula Junior car in 1958 in his Milan workshop. Similarly to most of his competing manufacturers, power was provided by a Fiat 1100 engine that was located in front of the driver, but unusually offset mounted, enabling the propeller shaft to pass alongside the driver, thus allowing a lower profile. Future development resulted in a rear engine layout and a choice of power plants between Fiat and DKW. Eventually, in recognition of technical advances, especially in Britain, a Ford Cosworth engine was installed.

Foglietti progressed into Formula 3 and Formula Ford, but by the end of the 1960s had ceased to manufacture cars.

Giaur/Giannini

During the 1920s, two brothers, Attilio and Domenico Giannini, set up Giannini Automobili SpA, and became a service centre for Itala, based in Rome. They became involved in motorsport, Giannini entering the first running of the Mille Miglia in 1927, driving an Itala Tipo 61, and won their class. During the 1930s the brothers started working on tuning small cars such as the Fiat 500 'Topolino,' leading to them developing racing cars, both single-seaters and sports, under their own name and using highly modified Fiat engines. In 1938, a Giannini, utilising a 500cc engine with a cylinder head modified by Siata, broke several world records.

Following the Second World War, and an unsuccessful foray into the transport sector, they concentrated on competition. A Giannini Spider finished second in class in the 1950 Mille Miglia. Some of their modified engines were linered down to 500cc and took part in the British Formula 3 series, but without success. The 1960s saw Giannini modified Fiat 500s competing against the Abarth versions, but with no great success. In more recent times, Giannini works with Fiat on servicing.

Giaur was formed in 1950 by the Giannini brothers in conjunction with Bernardo Taraschi who had built cars under the 'Urania' name; the name Giaur represented GIA from Giannini and UR from Urania. A typical Giaur is a two-seat sports car with a highly modified Fiat 750cc engine; it is believed that only 48 were made.

Gordini

Amédée Gordini was born in Bazzano, which is just outside the city of Bologna in Italy. As a youngster he had a fascination for motor cars and initially worked as a mechanic for Alfieri Maserati. After the First World War, when he had served in the Italian Army, he relocated to Paris. He then started to race Fiat cars, participating in most categories of racing, including the 24 hours of Le Mans. When Fiat launched the 508 Balilla in 1932, he started developing them for racing to the extent that, according to one magazine report, "practically every moving component in the engine was changed or modified, probably the only Fiat items left being the bore and stroke."

Henri Pigozzi, Fiat's representative in France, had a factory that started manufacturing Balillas under the 'Simca' name, was approached by Gordini. This relationship prospered to the extent that Gordini soon found himself head of the Simca racing department. It was here that, by demonstrating his skills at developing and improving basic engines, that he earned the nickname 'le sorcier de la mécanique' or in English 'the wizard mechanic.' The advent of the Tipo 508C with its 1100cc engine provided Gordini with further opportunities to weave his magic skills.

After the Second World War, Gordini produced a new 'monoposto' 1100cc Simca-Gordini, which incorporated a chassis and independent front suspension of his own design. Similarly to the Cisitalia D46, the new Simca-Gordinis were only competitive against other Grand Prix competitors on tight, twisty circuits where speed was secondary to agile handling. The break with Simca came as Gordini wanted to press ahead with more ambitious designs, but these were vetoed by Simca who still wanted him to concentrate on designs that incorporated many standard parts. As a result, at the end of 1951 they parted company and Gordini set up his own company.

Between 1952 and 1957 Gordini produced a variety of Grand Prix and racing sports cars, but like many small scale, specialist manufacturers he always suffered from a lack of adequate funding. With his motor racing ambitions finished, he was approached by Renault who gave him two decades of work in designing high-performance models from within their normal range. A hugely talented designer and engine tuner, Amédée Gordini passed away in 1979. His racing exploits are recorded in Chapters four and five.

OSCA

OSCA (Officine Specializzate Costruzione Automobili) was founded in 1947 by Ernesto Maserati and his two brothers Ettore and Bindo. During 1947 they left the Maserati firm they had founded in 1926, due to the fact that the company had been sold to Adolfo Orsi in 1937, but they had been given ten year contracts which expired that year. In addition to their racing activities (they had designed a 4½ litre Grand Prix car that was raced by Bira and Rol during 1951), they developed sports cars. Their first sports car was the MT4 (Maserati Tipo 4 cilindri) which had an 1100cc four-cylinder engine that utilised a Fiat derived block. The engine was developed and eventually enlarged to 1500cc, in which guise, driven by Stirling Moss and Bill Lloyd, an MT4 won the 1954 12-hours Sebring race.

As recounted in Chapter 7, in late 1959 OSCA introduced a Formula Junior car. It was of conventional design and incorporated an 1100cc Fiat engine mounted at the front. It was an attractive and well finished car that proved to be effective in the hands of Colin Davis.

The link with Fiat continued when in 1959 Fiat decided to fit the 1500cc OSCA engine to its 1500S coupé and convertible models. This engine was eventually increased

A 1951 Osca MT4 sports.

to 1600cc. OSCA was absorbed by the MV Agusta motorcycle company and the name disappeared from the automobile world.

Motto

Carrozzeria Rocco Motto was an Italian coach builder that specialised in aluminium bodywork. I have included the company here because it was extremely influential in several Fiat-based cars. Founded by Rocco Motto in 1932 after a spell with Martelleria Maggiora in Turin, where he learned his bodywork skills, he constructed bodies for major manufacturers such as Lancia. He also did work for other coachbuilders such as Ghia and Pininfarina. After the Second World War he began to specialise in lightweight aluminium bodies, especially for sports/racing cars. It is thought, although not proven, that he made bodies for the Fiat 508C Mille Miglia cars for Savio. Siata also commissioned Motto to build sports cars based on the Fiat 500 'Topolino' chassis.

When Cisitalia was set up after the Second World War, Giovanni Savonuzzi was appointed Technical Director on the recommendation of Giacosa Dante. Savonuzzi approached Motta and together they designed the Cisitalia D 46 racing car. Then an approach from Fiat led to a contract to manufacture the 1100S Berlinetta Mille Miglia; some 200 of these were produced by Motta until a contractual disagreement led to the contract being terminated. Motto also had close contacts with Nardi and built many bodies for him, most notably the Nardi 750. Motto continued to build special bodies for many manufacturers, including for Fiat-based specials such as Ermini, Siata, Bandini, Giaur, and Moretti.

Motto continued to work for many car manufacturers worldwide until in 1965, when in a major reappraisal of their work they turned to the production of caravans and commercial vehicle bodies.

Moretti

Another long established manufacturer of Fiat engine specials was Moretti. Founded in 1925 by Giovanni Moretti in Turin with the original intention of building motorcycles, but he started to build commercial vehicles during the Second World War, including electric powered small trucks. Once the war was over, he turned his attention to car production. Concentrating on Fiat-powered cars, the range not only included saloons, but also had coupés and single-seat racing cars. The 600 and 750 based saloons enjoyed some success during the 1950s. When Formula Junior was introduced in Italy, Moretti responded with a rear engine competitor, which was only partially successful (this is covered in more detail in Chapter 7).

Nardi

Enrico Nardi was a mechanic, engineer and driver who was born in Bologna in January 1907, but his family roots were in Turin and he eventually obtained a degree in Mechanical Engineering at the University of Turin. His first appointment was in the Test Office of Fiat and in 1930 he moved to Lancia where he became a test driver. In 1932, together with a former school friend, Augusto Monaco, he designed and built a racing car which used a British motorcycle engine, a JAP 998cc V twin. This car, called the 'Nardi-Monaco Chichibio,' was very successful in hillclimb events. The death of Vincenzo Lancia had a profound effect on Nardi, and he left Lancia, having accepted an offer from Enzo Ferrari to become test driver. At the time, Enzo Ferrari was managing the Alfa Romeo racing activities, and due to the overwhelming superiority of the German Silver Arrow teams, Mercedes-Benz and Auto Union, he was developing a voiturette car: the Alfa Romeo 158. On May 5, 1938 the car was driven for the first time, and the driver was Enrico Nardi. The Alfa Romeo 158 and its successor, the 159 went on to become the most successful Grand Prix cars after the Second World War, if not all time.

After the Second World War, Nardi produced the 750 Nardi-Danese as either a single-seat competition car or a two-seat sports car. Although it was assembled on a Fiat 500 chassis, it was powered by a 746cc BMW flat twin motorcycle engine. In fact, whilst Nardi utilised many Fiat components, very few, if any, were actually powered by Fiat-derived engines.

Nardi's main production in the early 1950s was accessories, which included tuning kits for Fiat 500 and 1100 engines. Later, towards the end of that decade, Nardi steering wheels became very popular. The production of the 750 continued, together with a number of specials powered by a variety of engines that included Lancia, Alfa Romeo and Panhard.

In 1953 Fiat introduced the new 1100/103TV and Vignale decided to produce a sports model based on the new Fiat, but decided that the engine needed improving and commissioned Nardi to undertake the required tuning. The result was the Fiat 1100 Nardi Vignale and some 60 were manufactured. In 1957 at the Geneva Motor Show a revised Fiat 1100/103 was displayed; the result of a joint effort between Nardi, Michelotti and Ghia, it was deemed a great success, but unfortunately due to financial problems at Ghia Suisse, it was the only one made. Allemano began selling upgraded Fiat 600s in 1957 with Nardi upgraded engines. An upgraded Fiat 600 engine also appeared in America in a Lotus XI chassis; although very successful in its class it was the only one produced. In 1959, Saragossa Nardi Espanola SA was established with the objective of producing the SEAT 600 Nardi, the SEAT 600 being the Fiat 600 manufactured in Spain.

On August 23, 1966, Enrico Nardi, who had been suffering from leukaemia, died in Turin. After his death the company struggled on for a time, but in 1970 his heirs sold the company and were no longer involved in the automotive business.

Raineri

The original Raineri Formula Junior car appeared at the very beginning of Formula Junior. It had the usual Fiat 1100 engine mounted at the front, and differed from most other designs due to its sharply tapered tail section, thereby exposing the Fiat 600-based rear suspension. Its Fiat engine was fed with fuel via two double-choke Weber carburettors. Its bodywork was also notable for its large air intake at the front. A later version appeared by the end of 1960 and was fitted with a Lancia Appia engine.

Siata

The 'Societa Italiana Auto Trasformazione Accessori,' otherwise known as Siata, was established in 1926 in Turin by former racing driver Giorgio Ambrosini. Initially, Siata sold modifications to tune Fiat cars. Following the Second World War, in 1948 Siata began the manufacture of motor cars under its own name. The first model, the Tipo P75, known as the 'Amica,' was a two-seater sports model that was available as a convertible (spider) or coupé. It was powered by either a 500cc or 750cc engine that was a modified Fiat 500 unit. A specially modified version of the Amica, known as the Fiat Siata Pescara, won the 1948 Italian Road Racing Championship, it had modified 500cc engine. It is thought that only two Pescaras were built and one survives today. The Amica was in production until 1952.

In 1950 a new model the 'Daina' was introduced. This was a sports cabriolet based on a modified Fiat 1400. The chassis was shortened and reinforced and there was a choice of three engine sizes, all Fiat-based: the 1.4L (1395cc), the 1.5L (1500cc) or the 1.8L (1817cc). It is estimated that some 50 Dainas were produced until 1958. Most of the production is thought to have been of the Gran Sport version, which was a cabriolet version, although the precise number is not known. In 1951, the 300BC Barchetta Sport Spider was introduced and, as the name implies, was an open, two-seat sports model.

Siata's involvement with the Fiat 8V ('Otto Vu'), as covered in Chapter 5, resulted in the Siata 208S which proved popular on race circuits, especially in the USA. In 1968 Siata launched the 'Siata Spring,' a small sports car based upon the Fiat 850 which continued in production until 1970, when Siata went bankrupt. Following Siata's demise, a new company, ORSA, took over production and based the Spring on the SEAT 850. The revised car stayed in production until 1975 when demand decreased drastically.

Stanguellini

The Officine Stanguellini Trasformazione Auto Corsa was established in 1936 in the city of Modena by Vittorio Stanguellini. The Stanguellini family had a long tradition in engineering and, in particular, relating to motor cars. Vittorio's father had the first car registered in Modena: a Fiat with the registration 'MO 1' can be seen in the Stanguellini museum in Modena.

Having already held a Fiat agency from the

A 1951 Siata 300 BC at the 2011 Mille Miglia.

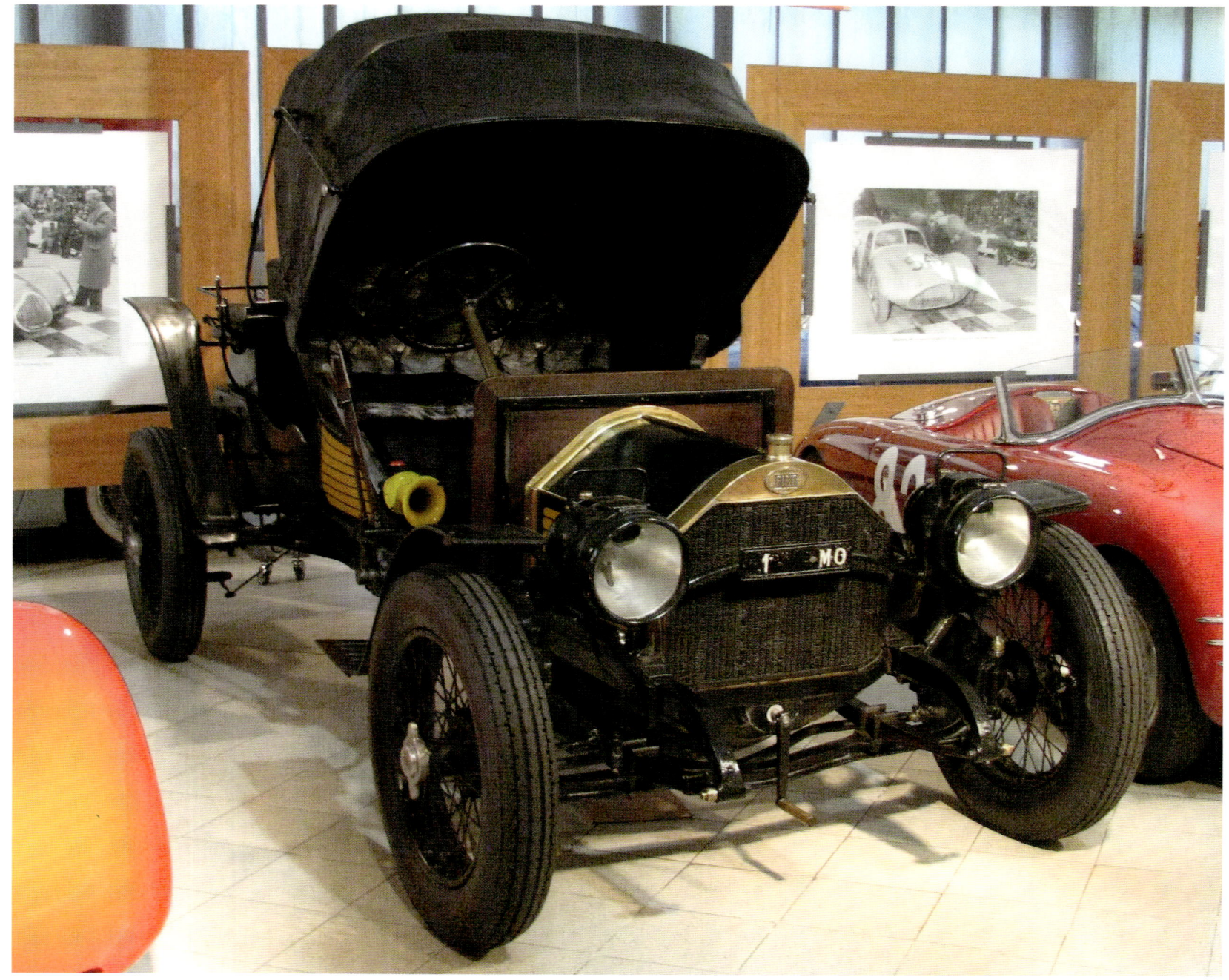

The first car registered in Modena – a very early Fiat.

1920s, the new company, in a similar manner to other specialist firms, started by tuning and modifying Fiat, Maserati and Alfa Romeo engines. Squadra Corsa Stanguellini, formed in 1938, was immediately successful with a Maserati 6CM.

After the Second World War, Stanguellini used his prewar experience to produce sports cars under his own name, utilising highly modified Fiat engines. He concentrated on the 750 and 1100cc classes and used as many Fiat parts as possible, eschewing the use of imported components where practical. Bodywork was usually by local carrozzieri. These cars achieved many notable class wins in major events such as the Mille Miglia and Targa Florio. In terms of road, rather than racing, cars, in 1947 Stanguellini produced a four-seat berlinetta utilising Fiat 1100 components and bodywork by Bertone. Later a Fiat 750-based two-seater was introduced.

Outside Italy, Stanguellini is probably best known for its Formula Junior race car. Looking very like a scaled-down Maserati

Left: A typical Stanguellini sports car in the Modena museum.

Below: A coupé in the Stanguellini museum —note the Fiat badge on the front.

Another example of a sports model in the Modena museum.

A Stanguellini Formula Junior car.

250F Grand Prix car, it was powered by a Fiat 1100 engine. One of the first manufacturers to support Formula Junior when it was introduced in 1958, the initial highly successful car was front-engined, and the dominant make in the early years of the formula. Over 100 were produced, and they won the inaugural Italian Formula Junior championship. Stanguellini's involvement in Formula Junior is covered in more detail in Chapter 7. The company withdrew from motor racing in 1967 and concentrated on tuning equipment, while still maintaining its Fiat agency in Modena. Today there is an excellent museum collection in its premises in Modena, and several Formula Junior cars still exist that are actively raced in appropriate events.

Taraschi

Bernardo Taraschi started building cars following the end of the Second World War. From 1947 until 1949 he built Urania sports cars based on Fiat 'Topolino' chassis and war surplus BMW motorcycle engines. He later utilised Giannini engines and participated in the formation of Giaur, as recorded earlier in this chapter.

Taraschi is probably better known for the Formula Junior cars he produced from 1959 to 1961. These cars had a front-engine design utilising the popular Fiat 1100cc engine. Some 63 are thought to have been built and, before the onslaught of the English rear-engined cars, were quite successful in Continental events, particularly in the hands of the English driver Colin Davis.

Volpini

Founded by Gianpolo Volpini in Milan in the late 1940s; the firm bearing his name initially started by building sports cars powered by the ubiquitous Fiat 1100 engine. These were raced through the 1950s until 1959, but without any conspicuous success. In 1952 a new Formula 3 car was launched; similar to the contemporary English contenders it was a rear engine design powered by a single cylinder 500cc Gilera motorcycle engine. In 1955, in conjunction with Egidio Arzani, Volpini constructed a Grand Prix car, the Arzani-Volpini. Although exceptionally well made for a 'one-off' special, it was not successful in its few appearances, the first of which was at Pau in France, where it

A Stanguellini Formula Junior car at Oulton Park. (Courtesy PMcF)

Another Stanguellini at Oulton Park. (Courtesy PMcF)

crashed, with fatal consequences for its young and inexperienced driver. Then, following the introduction of Formula Junior in 1958, Volpini, in a similar manner to many Italian specialist manufacturers, started constructing racing cars for the new category of racing. Similar in appearance to the Formula Junior Stanguellini, the Volpini was powered by a front-mounted Fiat 1100 engine enclosed in an aluminium bodyshell.

Wainer
The first Wainer car produced by Gianfranco Mantovani was a Fiat 1100 Formula Junior car that made its debut in 1958. Unusual at the time, it was a rear-engined design and, by using as many standard parts as possible, sold at a price that was considerably lower than its competitors.

Ron Hutchinson in a Wainer Formula Junior car at an event in Florida. (Courtesy DR)

Chapter Seven
Formula Junior

It was during October 1958 that the sporting committee of the Fédération Internationale de l'Automobile (FIA) approved Formula Junior for international recognition. As a result of this decision, events for these single-seat racing cars took place throughout Europe during 1959. However, it is necessary to retrace the developments that led to the decision to recognise this category of racing at international level. In 1956 the Italian Automobile Club (the governing body of motor racing in Italy) held a meeting at San Remo to discuss the shortage of up-and-coming Grand Prix drivers in Italy, and how to address this problem. Following much debate and consideration of a number of proposals, it was decided to adopt the suggestions of Count 'Johnny' Lurani, a well known driver and writer; he conceived a formula aimed at developing future Grand Prix drivers via a relatively inexpensive set of regulations (Count Lurani, with George Eyston, had won the 1100cc class in the 1933 Mille Miglia, driving a K3 MG Magnette). After Italy's leading drivers of the mid-1950s, Luigi Musso and Eugenio Castellotti, had both died on the race track, more impetus was added to his proposal.

The basis of the proposed formula was that it would comprise single-seater racing cars based on standard car components, and that engines should not exceed 1100cc. Clutches and gearboxes had to match the engine, and suspension and brakes had to come from the same model as the mechanical elements. There was also a minimum stipulated weight of 400kg. Due to the development of the Fiat 1100 engine by the various etceterini manufacturers, an ideal engine was immediately available. An alternative power plant was that of Lancia's V4 'Appia,' although this was more expensive than the Fiat unit. As recounted in the previous chapter, many of the Italian 'etceterini' manufacturers developed cars for this new category of racing.

The first race held for this new category was on April 25, 1958 at the Monza Autodrome, which was hosting the 6th Vigoreli Trophy meeting; the programme of races included a 12-lap event for 'Formula Junior and similar cars.' Cars from Stanguellini, Volpini, Taraschi, Raineri and Foglietti lined up for the start. All of these cars were Fiat powered and displayed considerable variety in their design. In the actual race, Roberto Lippi, driving a Stanguellini, took the chequered flag ahead of Taraschi, who was driving a car of his own design, and a Volpini. These three were the only cars to complete the race distance, and only two more finished after completing six and nine laps. This race demonstrated the unsuitability of the high-speed Monza circuit for these relatively low-powered cars. The next race took place on the much more suitable track at the Vallelunga parkland circuit in Rome. The race result mirrored the earlier event in respect of first and second cars and drivers, although on this occasion it was another Stanguellini in third place.

The next race was again held at Vallelunga and once again Lippi won, but this time second place went to Lucien De Sanctis driving a car of his own design. Taraschi finished third behind De Sanctis.

By June the new formula was attracting much support in Italy, helped, no doubt, by multiple World Champion Juan Fangio. Fangio's manager, Marcello Giambertone, establishing a service for Formula Junior drivers that once they had purchased a car and arrived at a circuit, the service team 'Scuderia Madunira,' would bring the cars, prepared by them, and provide a mechanic for the race, all of this at a cost. The rapidity with which this new formula was developing and attracting much support could be seen at Monza on June 29 when 23 cars were entered for a 15-lap race, the first Junior Cup, although only 19 actually started. Stanguellini was seen to be stamping its authority on this category of racing by taking the first four places. On this occasion, however, Lippi had to settle for second place, having been beaten by a promising newcomer by the name of Luigi Nobile.

At that time Formula Junior had not yet been granted international status, but during August a race was held at the Oporto circuit in Portugal as a precursor to the Portuguese Grand Prix. Scuderia Madunina sent a batch of cars for the race. Despite the presence of Italy's rising stars, the race was dominated by two Portuguese drivers who used local knowledge of the track to their advantage. As a result the winning car was driven by a local driver in yet another Stanguellini, with Nobile finishing in second place. Whilst undoubtedly the slippery tramlined surface of the circuit was a contributory factor, it was nevertheless impressive that the fastest lap of the Formula Junior race was only some 17mph slower than that of the actual Grand Prix. These diminutive cars were also proving their worth in hillclimbs, with Stanguellini and De Sanctis cars performing particularly well.

On September 8 a meeting was held at the Modena Autodrome, and yet again it proved to be a Stanguellini benefit, with Lippi winning both his heat and the final. The first non-Stanguellini finisher was a Volpini that finished in fourth place in both its heat and the final. The stranglehold that Stanguellini had over its competitors was finally broken on September 28 at Syracuse, when a Taraschi, driven by Luigi Zannini (Bernardo Taraschi was away racing at Modena), won from a Stanguellini driven by Gastone Zanarotti; Lippi had dropped out of his heat with mechanical problems. An unusual event was staged at Vallelunga on November 1; it was a team event based on a town-versus-town basis, the towns being Rome and Milan. Having participated in heats based on individual towns, the final took place and saw De Sanctis win from a close fought duel with Zannini in his Taraschi with the next four places occupied by Stanguellinis. There was then another race and the previous order was reversed with Zannini winning from De Sanctis. An interesting feature of the 'Rome race' was the appearance of future Grand Prix and sports car racer, Maria Teresa De Filippis.

Thus ended the first year of Formula Junior racing, which, apart from the Portuguese event and a race at Montlhéry (also won by a Stanguellini), had been confined to Italy. The leading make had undoubtedly been Stanguellini, but Taraschi and De Sanctis had also proved to be highly competitive, particularly towards the end of the year. It became obvious that the 1958 FIA, by granting International status to the new formula, provided the stimulus necessary to encourage manufacturers from other countries to develop appropriate cars. There were signs that Germany and France were ready to participate, and that England, if she chose to join in, would have suitable engines to use. Therefore the future looked bright for the new formula. The regulations framed by the FIA allowed for two maximum engine capacities, 1000cc or 1100cc plus an 88lb weight penalty for the larger engine cars.

Due to their experience during 1958, it was inevitable that the Italian manufacturers would start 1959 with an advantage, at least in the early stages. The early months of the year preceding the start of the 1959 season saw a flurry of announcements concerning new Formula Junior cars being manufactured, showing the increasing enthusiasm for the new formula. This situation didn't just apply to Italy, there were now new designs emerging from France, Austria and Germany, whilst interest was growing in Britain too.

January 1959 saw an unusual event take place at the Northern Italy ski resort of Cortina. This was Italy's first attempt at ice racing and attracted a healthy entry of Formula Junior cars, not just from Italy but also from France and Austria. Despite some shock defeats for the Italian contingent in the heats, won by Austrian Otto Mathè in his own designed car and Frenchman Gerard Laureau in a DB, the final was a victory for Manfredini in a Wainer, closely followed by Mathè and Laureau.

Further impetus was given to the new formula by the announcement in Italy that there was to be a Formula Junior International Championship. Initially, there were to be six qualifying rounds, two each from Italy, Germany and France. The points basis used was similar to that used for the drivers' World Championship, ie, eight points for a win, six for second, four for third, three for fourth and two for fifth place.

The 1959 season proper commenced in April at the Vallelunga circuit, and Lippi, who had been declared Formula Junior Champion of 1958, won both his heat and the 30-lap final. Lippi's win in the final was by no means a walkover, as Antonio Maglione driving a De Sanctis led for most of the race, only to retire with mechanical problems when almost in sight of the chequered flag. De Sanctis himself finished second with Englishman, Colin Davis, third in his Taraschi in what was his Formula Junior debut.

The next event, which was also to be the first championship round, was held at Monza on April 19. Sponsored by BP and organised by Scuderia Madunina, the race attracted 40 entries, although eventually only 35 appeared on the starting grid. A demonstration of Fiat's dominance in terms of power plants was the fact that, of the 35 starters, 33 were powered by variants of the Fiat 1100 or 1200 engines. Another interesting characteristic, was that 30 of the cars had the engine in front of the driver; a feature that was to change drastically in the near future. Stanguellini cars dominated both the heats and the final, which was run in two parts. Roberto Businello was the winner, Erasmo Crivellari second, and the first non-Stanguellini, a Taraschi driven by Davis, finished third.

Held at Cesanatico on the Italian Adriatic coast, the next race was 40 laps of the 1.7-mile course. An exciting race ensued with Frescobaldi, Lippi and Businello battling for the lead, eventually Piero Frescobaldi retired with brake problems, and Businello just managed to hold off Lippi to score yet another win. Sadly, Frescobaldi was to lose his life at Spa-Francorchamps in 1964. All three had been driving Stanguellinis, third and fourth places fell to a De Sanctis and a Taraschi respectively.

The next race was held at Monza, where the inadvisability of using this high speed circuit again became apparent, as out of 18 starters, only nine were classified as finishers. After the first five laps, eight cars had retired with four of these being eliminated in a first lap accident. Once again Stanguellini cars dominated proceedings, with Nino Crivellari beating Frescobaldi by the tiny margin of one tenth of a second. Swiss driver, Michael May, took third place in his Stanguellini. Future Grand Prix driver, Lorenzo Bandini finished fourth in a Volpini and a De Sanctis was fifth.

Following the Monza debacle, the somewhat depleted Italian FJ contingent travelled to Monaco for the first 'Grand Prix Monaco-Junior' and as a result Italian representation was limited to just six cars and faced a numerically superior French entry of nine cars. Four of the French entries were Stanguellini-based, with the remaining five consisting of Panhard-engined DBs and Monomills, plus two Renault-powered cars, a Rispal and a Ferry. Underlining the International status of the race, there were also single entries from Germany, Switzerland, Argentina and Britain. The three non-British cars were all Stanguellinis whilst the sole British entry was David Latchford driving a BMC A series-powered Halson. May took the lead from the start and held it throughout, eventually beating Giovanni Alberti to second place, with Juan Manuel Bordeu finishing third. All first three finishers were driving Stanguellinis, while Bandini finished fourth in his Volpini. So this race represented yet another overwhelming victory for Stanguellini, however this situation was soon to be overturned.

Immediately following the Monaco race, the Formula Junior 'circus' was at the Posillipo circuit at Naples. Driving a Taraschi, Davis won from Alfredo Tinazzo in a De Sanctis with another Taraschi in third place. The best that the Stanguellini contingent could achieve was fifth and sixth places, both cars having been lapped by the leader! One week later, Davis was able to repeat his previous performance at Pau in the south of France, on this occasion a Stanguellini driven by May managing to finish second, but only because Bordeu, also driving a Stanguellini, had spun earlier and was unable

Roberto Businello in his Stanguellini on his way to victory at Cesantico in April 1959. (Courtesy DR)

to catch May. On the same day there was also a six-hour race for Grand Touring and Formula Junior cars at Vallelunga. Alfredo Tinazzo, who sadly was to be fatally injured at Monza later in the year, was eventually victorious in his De Sanctis after a thrilling battle with Maglione, Renato Pirocchi and Lippi. Maglione was driving a De Sanctis, while both Pirocchi and Lippi were driving Stanguellinis.

The second round of the two French championship qualifying rounds took place at Albi on May 31 under the title the 'Albi Grand Prix;' this had previously been run under different formulae including Formula 1 and Formule Libre. In the final, only three cars managed to complete the full race distance, the winner being Davis in his Taraschi, followed by the Stanguellinis of Alberti and Gastone Zanarotti. This race marked the halfway stage in the 1959 Formula Junior Championship. The drivers' table showed May in the lead from Davis, Alberti and Bussinello. In the constructors' table, Stanguellini held a substantial lead over Taraschi, with Moretti and Volpini sharing third place.

At the same time as the Albi round was taking place, an event was being staged in Sicily on the fast road circuit at Pergusa. Raffaele Cammarota, driving a Stanguellini, led from start to finish; he was followed by two De Sanctis cars driven by Maglione and Tinazzo. Seven days later the ninth Circuit de Castello race took place, the programme consisting of two 10-lap heats followed by the 30-lap final. Taraschi and Maglione, who had both won their heats, shared the front row of the starting grid with Pirocchi. The result ended in Taraschi taking first place after an intense battle with Maglione and Pirocchi; however the latter pair both suffered problems, allowing Tinazzo into second place, followed by De Sanctis and Lippi. The next race was back in Sicily at the Caserta road circuit and Nino Crivellari in a Stanguellini won from Tinazzo in a De Sanctis.

The unsuitability of the ultra high-speed

Lorenzo Bandini in his Volpini at Pau in May 1959. (Courtesy DR)

Monza circuit for Formula Junior racing was once again brutally demonstrated on June 28. The Formula Junior race was a precursor to the 'Lottery Grand Prix for Grand Touring cars' and consisted of two 26-lap races, the winner being decided on the basis of aggregate times achieved over the two races. Fast and furious racing was anticipated, and so it proved to be, with unfortunate consequences. Up to that time, although the racing had become more competitive and aggressive, thankfully there had been only relatively minor incidents with no serious injuries, sadly this was about to change drastically. In the first race, there was a five car battle between Bordeu, May, Cammarota, Carmelo Genovese and Aquilino Branca. Bordeu, in his Stanguellini, won from Cammarotta and Genovese. However, on lap 21 Dino Montevago crashed at the Lesmo curve and suffered serious injuries after his Foglietti hit a tree, also crashing out was Zanarotti but thankfully without injury. Amid a fiercely fought race, on lap eight there was a multiple car crash when Tinazzo and Crivellari collided on the fast Vialone curve. Tragically both of these drivers lost their lives in the accident. Bordeu, having led from the start, won from Zanarotti and Cammarota. The aggregate result gave Bordeu victory from Cammarota and Frenchman Robert Revol; the first seven finishers were all driving Stanguellinis.

On July 12 the first Formula Junior event took place in Germany on the South circuit of the famous Nürburgring track. Due to a difference of opinion between the event organisers, the Germany Automobile Club (ADAC) and the Italians, there were no competitors from Italy. However, there was still an entry of 11 cars, of which six were Stanguellinis. Having taken the lead initially, 'Taffy' von Trips, the future Ferrari works driver, was passed by May who then led until his engine started to overheat, allowing

A Taraschi at Pau in May 1959. (Courtesy DR)

von Trips to retake the lead which he then held until the finish. May managed to keep going and finished second, in front of Gerhard Mitter in his two-stroke Mitter-DKW.

The next race was held two weeks later, once again in Germany, but on this occasion at the Solitude circuit near Stuttgart. Italian drivers were again absent, but the 18 starters included nine who were driving Stanguellinis. In the race itself, May and Bordeu battled throughout until Bordeu's engine expired. This let May win comfortably, whilst the unfortunate Bordeu eventually pushed his car over the finishing line and was credited with sixth place.

Returning to Italy on August 22/23, a ten-hour meeting was held at Messina which included a 20-lap Formula Junior race. In addition to its regular drivers, the Stanguellini contingent included two new names, Fritz D'Orey and Biro Heinz, both of whom were from Brazil, demonstrating how Formula Junior was now attracting world-wide interest and support. The race developed into a battle between D'Orey and Cammarota, until the latter spun due to his right foot being trapped between the accelerator and brake pedals, allowing Heinz up into second place. Cammarota eventually managed to work

his way back up the field, and was in third place behind the two Brazilians by the end of the race. Being the first Italian driver to finish, Cammarota had now put himself into a position to challenge for the Italian National Formula Junior Championship, the previous leader, Tinazzo, having perished in the tragic Monza race in June.

The Eife Pokal races were held on the South circuit of Nürburgring on August 30. With a full field which, on this occasion, comprised all the leading drivers, including those from Italy, it was nevertheless another Stanguellini benefit with Swiss driver May taking the honours from fellow Stanguellini driver, Pirocchi, whilst a German driven DKW-engined car was third. Interestingly, the increasing British interest in the new formula was demonstrated by the fact that Bill de Selincourt brought a BMC A-series engined Elva Junior into fourth place.

Elvas featured in the next Formula Junior race held at the French circuit of Cadours. Entered by R (Dick) Fitzwilliam, who had now increased his team to two cars, they were to be driven by de Selincourt and Fitzwilliam himself. Run in two heats and then a final, de Selincourt stunned the opposition by winning his heat decisively and then, in the final, having battled for the lead with May and D'Orey, won after the latter had problems with his throttle pedal. Second, third and fourth places were taken by Stanguellinis, with May leading the group. Thus, Bill de Selincourt became the first British driver to win an International Formula Junior race in a British car.

Back in Italy, Vallelunga held its last race of the year. On this occasion Maglione's De Sanctis car proved reliable, and enabled him to win, beating Lippi into second place, followed home by Pirocchi and Bandini. Although it wasn't known at the time, the next event would decide the outcome of that year's Italian National Formula Junior Championship. The event in question was the ninth Gold Cup race held at Syracuse in Sicily. Cammarota, Bandini and Pirocchi led from the start with the former leading initially, only to be passed by Pirocchi, closely followed by Bandini. Then Bandini took the lead, only to be immediately re-passed by Pirocchi but then Cammarota made his challenge with only three laps to go, and won. Pirocchi and Bandini finished second and third respectively. As a result of this race result, Raffaele Cammarota became Italian National Formula Junior Champion for 1959 and Stanguellini was the top make again.

There was still one race to take place before the 1959 season ended: the Madunina Cup meeting held at Monza on November 22. It had been scheduled to take place one week earlier but had to be postponed due to bad weather. Due to the tragic accidents earlier in the year, a new loop was built within the road circuit part of the track. This alteration enabled Formula Junior and production car races to take place without using the high speed banked section of the original circuit. The racing was as fiercely fought as usual, but thankfully on this occasion with no serious accidents. Bandini was in excellent form, winning both his heat and the final in his Stanguellini. 'Geki' (a pseudonym for Giacomo Russo) was second, and Nicoletti third. The new loop had certainly proved effective in making the racing safer, but no less competitive.

Thus ended the first year of the Formula Junior International Championship. The racing had been close, sadly with some fatalities; clearly the engine that had proved to be the most competitive was the Fiat 1100 and the most successful manufacturer was Stanguellini. However, during the year, whilst Britain had not been prominent on the International scene, interest was increasing and there had been a number of local events. Initially, the Formula Junior entries had not been competitive against even the Formula 3 cars but that was slowly changing. BMC A-series powered cars such as Elva, Moorland and Gemini were proving successful. Towards the end of the year several new cars appeared, first the Cooper, BMC-powered as the earlier cars, then Lola which took a different route utilising a Ford power unit, and finally Colin Chapman with a Ford 105E-powered car. Thus the scene was set to mount a serious challenge to the previous domination by Fiat-powered cars. Lola had installed a Coventry Climax Formula 2 engine simply to test the prototype, which was clearly not Formula Junior eligible.

A number of events were held in Britain early in 1960, and one race in particular gave a foretaste of what was to come. At Oulton Park in Cheshire on April 2, there was a Formula Junior race in the programme, the main event being a Formula 2 race. This was the first time that the latest British Formula Junior cars faced a Stanguellini. The Italian car was completely outclassed and trailed round at the tail of the field.

The 1960 International season started with a race in Cuba! There was now a new Formula Junior World Trophy and the Cuban race was a qualifying event. The event comprised two races held four days apart, one being the Havana Grand Prix and the other the Liberty Grand Prix. As the final result was based upon the aggregate times from each race, drivers were concerned that if they failed to complete one race they wouldn't score any championship points. Their fears were well grounded in that this is precisely what happened. In race one, American driver Peter Carpenter won after Bandini and Lippi had to retire, the first nine cars were all Stanguellinis. The second race was won by Bandini, but due to his failure to finish in the previous race he scored no points. By virtue of his finishing fourth in the first race and third in the second, Melarosa was declared the winner.

Before the European season started there had been a Formula Junior race in Florida that supported the 12-hour Sebring race. To the consternation of the Stanguellini entrants, a Cooper led by a considerable margin until engine problems sidelined it. In Europe on April 10, the season 'opener' took place at Vallelunga and proved to be a good day for De Sanctis, with Maglione winning from the Stanguellini driven by Pirocchi, who was followed by the De Sanctis of Lippi.

The increasing threat posed by the British manufacturers was demonstrated a week later at Cesenatico where two Coopers were entered. This was the first occasion that Britain's latest Formula Junior cars faced the European contenders on their home ground. The Coopers were driven by Dutchman Rob Slotemaker and American Carroll Smith. The race was run in two heats and a final. Slotemaker comfortably won his heat, while Stanguellini driver, Zanarotti, won his. However, in the final, Smith, having his first drive, and having finished fourth in his heat, gradually worked his way through the field to take the lead on the last lap which he then held to the finish.

The second round of the World Championship took place at Monza on April 24. The race, which was for the Vigorelli Trophy, comprised three heats and two finals, the winner being based on the aggregate times in the two finals. In addition to two Coopers, the British contingent now included three Lolas, but significantly for the Italian enthusiasts there were also some examples of the new OSCA car, these being Fiat-powered. The first heat saw another win for a Cooper, the second was a virtual Stanguellini walkover with only Facetti driving his own design, Lancia-powered car, spoiling a clean sweep by Stanguellini by finishing second. The third heat was won by another Lancia-powered car – a Dagrada, driven by Giancarlo Baghetti. The two finals gave Baghetti overall victory, as his main challenger Davis had retired in the first leg of the final. The next three places were filled by Stanguellinis.

Enrico Martin in his Foglietti at Cesenatico in April 1960. (Courtesy DR)

The third round of the Championship was held on May 29 at Monaco as a precursor to the Grand Prix proper. This turned out to be the clearest indication so far as to the impact the British manufacturers were now exerting on this category of racing. With a significantly oversubscribed entry for the race, in which only 22 cars were allowed to take part, qualifying was extremely important. In the event, out of the 22 starters only six non-British cars qualified, which comprised one OSCA, one De Sanctis and four Stanguellinis. In the race, Jim Clark led for most of the race until his Lotus started to misfire, dropping him back. Eventually, Henry Taylor won in his Ken Tyrrell entered Cooper. At the finish the highest non-British finisher was May in 10th place in his Stanguellini.

Then a number of events in Britain took place, all of which were dominated by local manufacturers. A Formula Junior race followed at Chimay in Belgium, and once again the British teams dominated, with a Lola driven by Southern Rhodesian John Love the winner. The next Championship round took place at Albi in France in June, and saw the Cooper Team of Henry Taylor and Ian Raby finish first and second in the final, with the best placed Stanguellini driven by Davis in fourth place.

The first half of the 1960 season ended with the Lottery Grand Prix at Monza. Some controversial decisions by the scrutineers resulted in the Lotus and Lola teams being excluded, leaving only the Cooper team and a solitary Elva to face the continental opposition. The usual format of two heats and a final was followed. The final saw a runaway win for Davis in his OSCA, after two of the Coopers were involved in a collision. Henri Grandsire brought his Stanguellini into second place and New Zealander, Dennis Hulme, was third in another Cooper.

There was a Formula Junior race at Rheims in France on 3rd July. Rheims was a flat and fast circuit that, like the original Monza circuit, was not suited to this category of racing. However, the racing was close and run in two heats with the winner decided on the aggregate times for the heats. It was another very successful day for the British teams, the winner being Mike McKee in a Lotus. The first four places were taken by British cars. Two races took place in Germany at the Nürburgring and Solitude, neither of which were championship rounds and both resulted in victory for British teams.

There was a race at Salerno in Sicily which was run under the normal format of two heats and a final. The heats were won by Hulme in his Cooper and Davis in his OSCA respectively. In the final, the OSCA driven by Davis won

Grand Prix Junior – Monaco 1961, Raffaele Cammarota in his De Sanctis. (Courtesy DR)

comfortably from Hulme, with Taraschi third. The next championship round took place in Sicily at Messina and was titled the Messina Grand Prix. The result of the heats reflected the Salerno positions, although on this occasion Davis was driving a Taraschi rather than his now usual OSCA. Once again Hulme finished runner-up, well clear of the rest of the field.

There were several Formula Junior races in Britain before the next round of the World Trophy took place, all of the British races being dominated by locals with no intervention by overseas makes. The next Championship round took place in July at Pescara in Italy. The race, given the title of 'Pescara Grand Prix,' followed the usual format of two heats followed by the final. Following an exciting duel between Davis and Hulme, the latter won after Davis spun off on the last lap. Second place went to Bordeu in a Stanguellini, with Love third in another Cooper. Although Formula Junior racing was thriving at national level, it was not until October that the remaining rounds of the World Trophy took place. The first was at Klagenfurt in Austria and, due to a date clash with the Junior Cup race being held at Monza on the same day, it attracted a mainly local entry. Gerhard Mitter, driving a Lotus powered by an Auto-Union engine, won from Kurt Ahrens Jr in a Stanguellini. Ahrens was to become German Formula Junior champion the following year. As none of the leaders had scored any points in previous rounds of the World Trophy, this result had no effect on the drivers' standing in the points table.

The Monza event, incorporating the Junior Cup, attracted a mainly Italian entry. The usual format of two heats and a final was adopted. In the heats, the works Stanguellinis showed an improved performance and won both heats. Surprisingly, Davis' OSCA could not match the speed of the Stanguellinis, nor that of the Wainer. In the final, bad weather intervened with the result that Manfredini was able to take advantage of the superior handling of the Wainer and won from Davis' OSCA and Baghetti's Lancia-powered Dagrada.

The final round of the 1960 World Trophy took place at Syracuse on October 23. The race, titled the 'Golden Cup,' was won by Davis in his OSCA, thus cementing his position as World Trophy holder of 1960. In second place came Frenchman Jacques Cales, in his Stanguellini, a result that placed him second in the World Trophy. Thus ended the first World Trophy series for Formula Junior competitors. Behind Davis and Cales came Hulme, Bandini, Grandsire and Trevor Taylor. It was now clear that the Fiat-powered Stanguellinis were no longer enjoying the superiority of the previous season.

The 1961 season demonstrated quite dramatically that the domination of Fiat-powered cars was over, and that the British constructors, in particular Cooper and Lotus, were now the most successful entrants. In fact out of some 43 Formula Junior races during the year, only five were won by Fiat-powered cars. This includes two each for Stanguellini and De Sanctis and one for a Fiat-powered Cooper. The advent of the new 1961 Grand Prix formula for cars with 1500cc engines also had a significant impact on Formula Junior, with the result that the last events took place in 1963, being replaced by new Formula 2 and Formula 3 categories.

CHAPTER EIGHT
Rallying: Fiat Returns

Chapter nine will recall the Abarth/Fiat connection and its implications, but for this chapter the story begins at the time of Fiat's takeover of Abarth, which was intended to prevent the latter from going into liquidation. When the 124 Sport Spider, designed by Pininfarina and styled by Tom Tjaarda, was introduced in 1966, it seems extremely unlikely that management at Fiat could foresee the successful career the car had in front of it, both in terms of the race track and rallies. In fact by 1969 the 124 was already being rallied by private owners to some effect. In 1970 the 1600cc version driven by Alcide Paganelli and Nino Russo won that year's Italian Championship.

On completion of the merger with Abarth, Fiat established a separate racing division at the Abarth premises at Corso Marche in Turin, the city where Fiat was founded in 1899, and remained the centre of car manufacture for the company. Thus the official Fiat rally/racing team was founded, initially utilising Fiat 125S saloons and 124 Sport Spiders.

The 125 saloons were uncompetitive and scored few, if any, victories. However, the 124 Sport Spiders were more successful, achieving wins on the Island of Elba and Costa Brava rallies; in the former event 124s were successful on two occasions. In 1972 a Spider also won the tough Acropolis Rally at its debut, and in the Rallye de Portugal Paganelli/Russo finished in fifth place overall.

At the end of 1972, the 124 was renamed as the Fiat 124 Abarth Rally and was subjected to further development which included increasing the engine size to 1756cc (the original model having been 1438cc, increased to 1600cc by 1970) and a resultant increase in power to 128hp. For Group 4 rallying purposes, however, the power output eventually reached 170hp. In order to qualify for Group 4, production volumes had to be at least 400 units, amongst other criteria, and Abarth achieved this before the end of 1972. Whilst the original 124 Spiders had been run in open-top configuration, the Abarth Rally versions always ran with a permanent hardtop in place.

1973 was the first year of the new World Rally Championship, and the first round was the Monte Carlo Rally. Unfortunately, this event, as several years earlier, was marred by controversy. The weather was appalling and as many as 20 cars were disqualified due to becoming stuck in snow drifts that were caused by the way the snow had been cleared. Later some 100 cars were also disqualified due to their failure to achieve the required times, despite this being due to the delays behind the cars trapped in snow drifts. As a result, out of the 278 cars that started, only 51 qualified as finishers! Alpine Renaults dominated the results, but in seventh place came a 124 Abarth Rally driven by Raffaelle Pinto/Arnaldo Bernacchini. In the Acropolis Rally, Rauno Aaltonen/Robin Turvey finished in second place, and another 124 Rally came fourth. There was an outright win in Poland for Achim Warmbold, while Maurizio Verini/Angelo Torriani took second place at San Remo. All of these results were achieved in the 124 Abarth Rally models.

For the 1974 season the engines had been equipped with 16-valve cylinder heads and the power increased to 200hp. There was no Monte Carlo rally this year due to the fuel crisis that arose out of the Arab/Israeli conflict. The first success for the revised car came at its debut in the TAP Rallye de Portugal when Pinto/Bernacchini won from their teammates Paganelli/Russo, followed by Markku Alén/Ilkka Kivimaki. In the Rally of 1000 Lakes, Alén/Kivimaki finished third, with another 124 in sixth place. Whilst success eluded them in the East African Safari Rally, Robin Ulyate/Ivan Smith did manage to bring their car home in tenth place. Further development included the installation of Kugelfischer fuel-injection equipment in

Abarth factory showing the 124 production line. (Courtesy GR)

A 124 Spider wins on its debut in the 1972 Acropolis Rally. (Courtesy FCA)

FIAT IN MOTORSPORT SINCE 1899

Verini/Torriani finished second in the 1973 San Remo Rally. (Courtesy FCA)

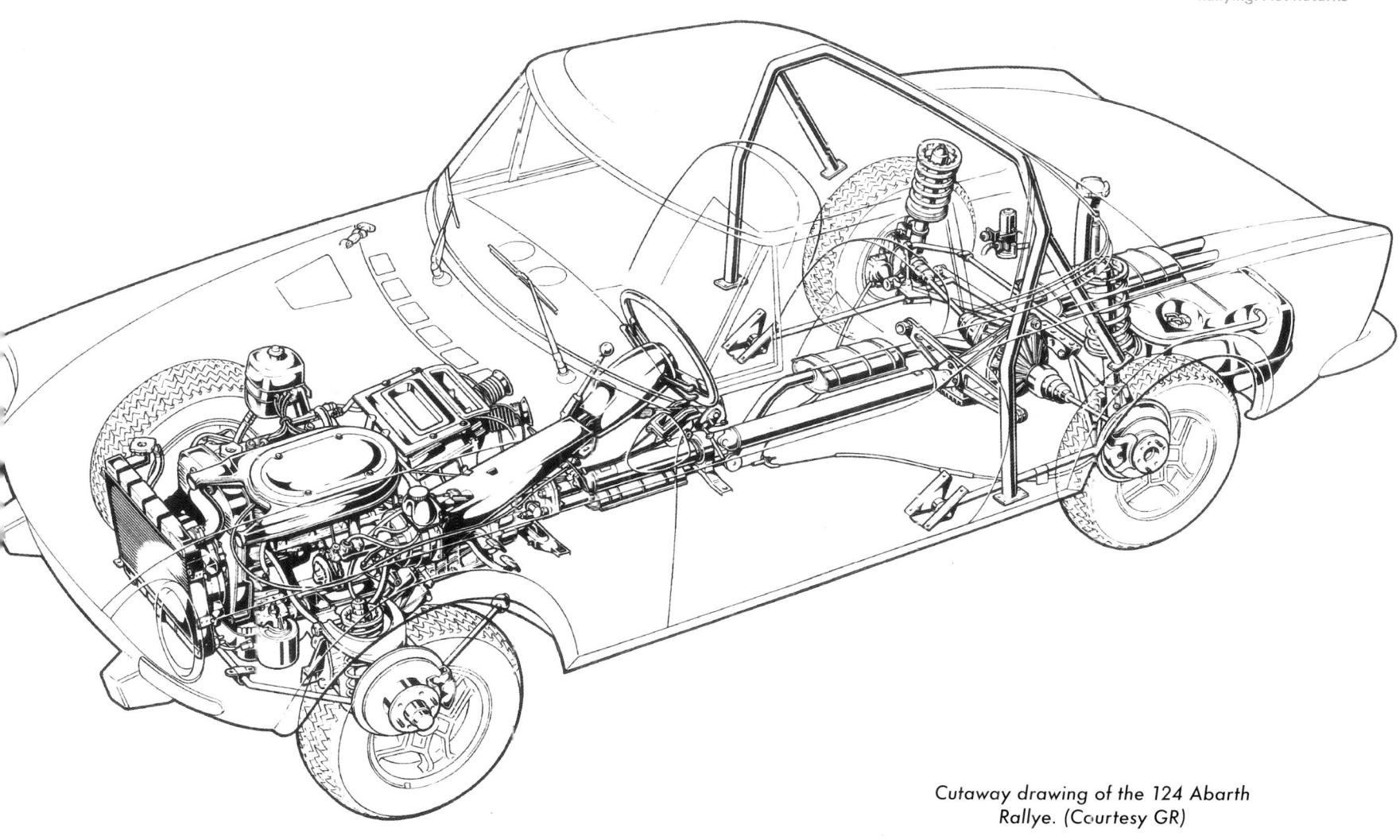

Cutaway drawing of the 124 Abarth Rallye. (Courtesy GR)

place of the previous Weber carburettors, which further increased the power output to 215hp. In the San Remo Rally, Giulio Bisulli/Francesco Rosetti finished second, but the rest of the team were eliminated through accidents.

Following the fiasco of the 1973 event, the 1975 Monte Carlo rally attracted only 96 starters, compared to the 278 of the previous event. The improvements carried out earlier helped the 124 Abarth Rallys of Hannu Mikkola/ Jean Todt to take second place overall; they were followed home by teammates Alén/ Kivimaki and Fulvio Bacchelli/Scabini in third and fourth places.

Only two works cars were entered for the Arctic Rally in Finland, one retired, but Mikkola/ Todt managed to finish, albeit only in seventh place having been soundly beaten by Saab. Alén/Kivimaki then went on to win the Rallye de Portugal, while in second place came the sister car of Mikkola/Todt.

In the RAC Rally, Maurizio Verini/Rossetti finished in eighth place and in the Swedish Rally, fifth and sixth places were the best the team could achieve. The Rally Costa Brava saw a clear victory for Verini/Rossetti, with fellow team colleagues, Bacelli/Scabini retiring, but a Polski Fiat entry finished in fifth place. In the Moroccan Rally, however, all three of the Fiat team cars retired. Verini won the 1975 European Rally Championship driving a 124 Abarth. Due to the success of the 124, Fiat was second to Lancia in the World Rally Championship, which at that time only related to manufacturers.

The final result for the 1976 Monte Carlo Rally saw the usual clean sweep by the Lancia Stratos, but in one of the last, if not *the* last, appearances of a works 124, Alén/Kivimaki finished in sixth place overall with Cambiaghi/ Scabini in eighth place. Another sixth place was achieved by Livio Lorenzelli in that year's San Remo rally. Fiat's attention had for some time switched to developing the 131 saloon as a rally car, and its works team of 124 Abarth Rally cars was disbanded. However, before recalling Fiat's experiences in rallying with the 131, there is another episode which merits recording.

Since the late 1960s Fiat had considered developing a sports car to complement its existing range. The new 128 range had been announced in 1969 and the 850 Spider continued to be built; in fact it only ceased production in 1973. Utilising the 128 overhead camshaft engine, but mounted at the rear,

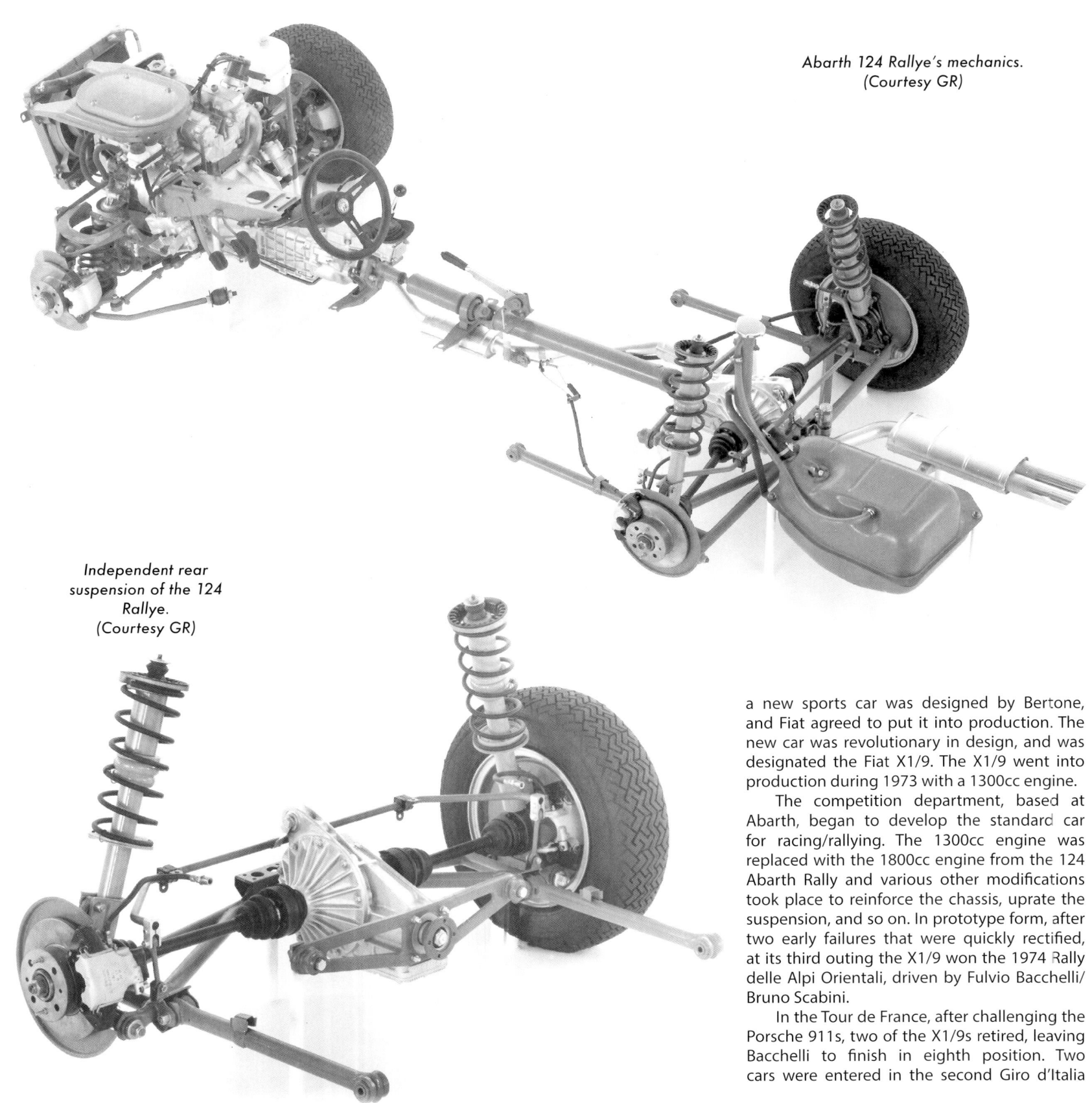

Abarth 124 Rallye's mechanics. (Courtesy GR)

Independent rear suspension of the 124 Rallye. (Courtesy GR)

a new sports car was designed by Bertone, and Fiat agreed to put it into production. The new car was revolutionary in design, and was designated the Fiat X1/9. The X1/9 went into production during 1973 with a 1300cc engine.

The competition department, based at Abarth, began to develop the standard car for racing/rallying. The 1300cc engine was replaced with the 1800cc engine from the 124 Abarth Rally and various other modifications took place to reinforce the chassis, uprate the suspension, and so on. In prototype form, after two early failures that were quickly rectified, at its third outing the X1/9 won the 1974 Rally delle Alpi Orientali, driven by Fulvio Bacchelli/Bruno Scabini.

In the Tour de France, after challenging the Porsche 911s, two of the X1/9s retired, leaving Bacchelli to finish in eighth position. Two cars were entered in the second Giro d'Italia

Aaltonen/Turvey finish second in the 1973 Acropolis Rally. (Courtesy GR)

Portugal 1974 – Alén/Kivimaki finish third. (Courtesy FCA)

Tenth place in the 1974 East African Safari Rally. (Courtesy FCA)

Automobilistico, but both suffered engine failures. Success came again when Bacchelli/Scabini won the Rally 10,000 Trabucchi during October. However, as Bertone was preparing to begin production to meet the homologation requirements of Group 4, management at Fiat took the decision not to proceed, and to concentrate its efforts on developing the 131 for rallying. Introduced in 1974, the 131 was a straightforward, four-door family saloon with a choice of either a 1300cc or 1600cc engine.

A 131 fitted with a 3.5-litre V6 engine, described as an Abarth SE 031 was entered in Group 5 of the 1974 Giro d'Italia event, where Giorgio Pianta/Bruno Scabini finished second. The following year Pianta drove the 031 into first place in the Giro d'Italia. Also in 1975, Fulvio Baccelli/ Scabini won the Rally delle Valli Piacentine in the same car. Meanwhile, Pianta had been appointed as lead engineer on 131 Abarth project. His appointment came about due to the tragic death of Mike Parkes in a road accident near Turin.

The Fiat Group embraced Lancia in its portfolio of companies and therefore was closely associated with the Lancia Stratos rally car that had enjoyed phenomenal success in international rallying, being World Rally Champion for Manufacturers in 1974, 1975 and 1976. The decision to utilise the 131 saloon as the basis for its rally effort was based upon the principle of the publicity impact of what appeared on the surface to be a normal saloon that anyone could purchase. This had been amply demonstrated by the Ford Escort in rallying, and the boost in sales attributed to the success of this model.

So, in 1975, Abarth embarked on the 'Fiat 131 Abarth Rally programme.' The two-door bodyshell was used, but, unlike the standard model, extensive use of glass-fibre enabled the weight to be kept down to 930kg. As with the 124 Abarth Rally, initially the engine was 1800cc, but that was soon replaced with the 2000cc version. Again similar to the 124, Kugelfischer fuel-injection was used, which increased the power output to 215hp. It is generally acknowledged that the 131 handled better than an Escort or a Stratos, due to the suspension based upon MacPherson struts and, with the rear end geometry revised, the system worked well, with dampers being the only problem areas. The complexity of the reworked bodyshells, utilising fibreglass, aluminium

Paganelli/Russo eventually retire in the 1974 San Remo Rally. (Courtesy GR)

Giorgio Pianta wins the 1975 Giro d'Italia in the Fiat-Abarth SE031. (Courtesy FCA)

1975 Monte Carlo Rally Mikkola/Todt in second place. (Courtesy GR)

Bacchelli/Scabini came fourth in the 1975 Monte Carlo Rally. (Courtesy GR)

Alén/Kivimaki taking third place in the 1975 Monte Carlo Rally. (Courtesy GR)

Markku Alén

Markku Alén was born on February 15, 1951 in Helsinki, Finland. His father was a Finnish champion in ice racing, which fostered an interest in motorsport in the young Markku. He started in rallying in 1969, driving a Renault 8 Gordini, and finishing ninth in the 1000 Lakes Rally at his first attempt. The Finnish Volvo importer then contracted him to drive a Volvo 142. With this car he finished third in the 1000 Lakes Rally in both 1971 and 1972, and second, to Timo Mäkinen, in 1973, when it was a round of the World Rally Championship for the first time. His performances in his home rally brought him to the attention of both Ford and Fiat.

Driving a Ford Escort RS 1600, Markku finished third in the 1973 RAC Rally behind Timo Mäkinen and Roger Clark. This result, despite having rolled his car and dropping to 178th place, led to Fiat contracting him for its rally team. For the two years, 1974 and 1975, Markku drove the Fiat 124 Abarth Rally with considerable success. He had several podium finishes, but they were eclipsed by his result in the 1975 Rallye de Portugal where he finished first: his first World Rally Championship victory.

The following year Fiat launched the Fiat 131 Abarth Rally, and Markku immediately made an impact in this new car. With it he won the 1976 1000 Lakes Rally and subsequently seven more World Championship events. He was instrumental in Fiat gaining the World Rally Championship for Manufacturers in 1977 and 1978. Having given the Fiat 131 its first victory in the 1976 1000 Lakes Rally, Markku also gave the car its last ever victory in a World Championship event in Portugal in 1981. Markku, together with his co-driver Ilkka Kivimaki, was undoubtedly the single most successful team in the Fiat 131 Abarth team.

He also enjoyed driving the Lancia Stratos rally car, winning the 1978 Rallye San Remo, which together with his Fiat 131 victories that year resulted in him winning the FIA Cup for Drivers, plus, of course, the manufacturers' championship for Fiat. When the Fiat 131 Abarth Rally team was disbanded, Markku moved across to the Lancia team, which of course was then owned by Fiat. He then drove the new Lancia Rally 037 and helped Lancia win the 1983 World Championship for Manufacturers. Following the withdrawal of the 037 from front line rallying, Markku continued to drive for Lancia, first in the Lancia Delta S4 and then in the Lancia Delta Integrales.

After Lancia had withdrawn from rallying in 1990, Markku drove for Subaru and Toyota until he retired from front line rallying in 1993. However, he didn't disappear completely, periodically competing in touring cars and the odd rally.

In a wonderfully successful career as a rally driver, Markku Alén won no fewer than 20 World Championship events. Sadly he never managed to win the World Championship for Drivers, although he came close on several occasions.

Seventh place for Mikkola/Todt in the 1975 Arctic Rally. (Courtesy GR)

Alén/Kivimaki in sixth place in the 1975 Swedish Rally. (Courtesy FCA)

and steel, and Perspex side windows, plus the disruption that would be caused by inserting a short-run special project into a high volume mass production line, made the model unsuitable for production at Fiat's main plant at Mirafiore (the standard 131 was known as the '131 Mirafiore'), so Bertone was commissioned to rework the standard bodyshells. Abarth also lacked the facilities required to produce the 400 needed for Group 4 homologation. There were marked differences between the 400 production road cars and the fully tuned works rally cars, an example being carburation, where the road cars had a single downdraught twin-choke Weber 34 ADF unit and the works cars had either two vertical twin-choke Weber 48 IDF units or Kugelfischer fuel-injection. Homologation was achieved by April 1976 and three cars were immediately entered in the Elba Rally that took place that month. One car retired with gearbox failure, but the remaining two finished in first and second places; it has to be said that this victory was achieved in part due to the failure of the main opposition, however it was a win on the car's first competitive outing. The winning drivers were Alén/Kivimaki, followed by Bacchelli/Rosetti in second place.

The fifth round of the 1976 World Championship took place in Morocco on June 22-27, and saw the debut of the 131 on the international stage. Unfortunately, it wasn't a glorious debut as two of the three cars retired, and the other one, driven by Alén/Kivimaki, struggled on through numerous problems to finish in 12th place. However, it was all change at the next championship round in Finland in August. Alén, partnered as usual by Kivimaki, won after a storming drive in the '1000 Lakes' rally that took place at the end of August. Then in October it was the Italian round of the championship held at San Remo, when Fiat entered a team of four cars for what was its home event. Sadly, it wasn't Fiat's day, as all four cars retired due either to mechanical failures or accidents.

In preparation for the 1977 season, Fiat spent the winter of 1976/77 sorting out the various issues that had affected the 131's reliability during the previous year. The first event of the season was the Monte Carlo Rally held on January 22-28, and, as expected, was dominated by a Lancia Stratos, on this occasion driven by Sandro Munari. However, despite three out of the four 131s entered failing for

The 1975 Moroccan Rally. (Courtesy GR)

various reasons, the Fiat France entry, driven by Jean-Claude Andruet and his female co-driver Michele Espinos-Petit, known as 'Biche,' finished in second place, therefore gaining some valuable championship points for the Italian manufacturer. The next championship round took place on February 11-13, in Sweden. For Fiat it was a disastrous event with all three team cars retiring due to reliability issues, this was particularly disappointing as Timo Mäkinen, having his first drive for the team, was in second place for much of the event until electrical problems caused his retirement.

After the disastrous Swedish event, the team went to Portugal during March with three cars entered, plus a lone entry from Fiat France. The actual rally saw an exciting struggle between Alén and Björn Waldegård, who was driving a works Ford Escort RS1800. In the end it was Alén, accompanied as usual by Kivimaki, who triumphed, thereby giving the Fiat 131 Abarth Rally its first World Championship victory. Team mates Andruet/'Biche' and Verini/Rosetti finished in fourth and fifth places respectively. Only Bacchelli/Rosetti failed to finish due to their car having suffered damaged suspension. The next championship event was the Safari Rally, which Fiat decided against entering, presumably due to the extremely harsh conditions normally experienced there.

May 1 saw the start of the South Pacific Rally held in New Zealand, and Fiat had its usual three-car team. All of the works team cars had problems, but amazingly, Bacchelli/Rosetti crossed the finishing line in first place, the car running on only three cylinders! Team mates Alén/Kivimaki and Simo Lampinen/Andresson Sölve finished in third and fourth places respectively, only Ari Vatinen's second place in a Ford Escort RS 1800 prevented a Fiat clean sweep!

The Acropolis Rally in Greece was the next championship round and took place between May 28 and June 3. Compared to the excellent result in New Zealand, in Greece the best the Fiats could achieve was the fourth place attained by Lampinen/Sölve, the rest having retired with driveshaft failure. Ford now decided, that having won both the Safari and Acropolis rallies, it would contest all the remaining championship rounds, thus presenting Fiat with serious competition.

The next championship round was the Rally of 1000 Lakes held in Finland between

A 124 practice car, venue unknown. (Courtesy FCA)

Left: Typical 131 Abarth Rally engine bay. (Courtesy GR)

Bottom left: The somewhat full boot of a 131 Abarth Rally. (Courtesy GR)

August 26-28. Fiat entered five cars, including one for a newcomer to the team, Timo Salonon, partnered by Jaakko Markkula. In the event it was newcomer, Salonen, who upheld Fiat's honour by finishing second, splitting the Ford Escort RS1800s of Hämäläinen and Waldegård. Markku Alén had led for much of the rally, only to be sidelined after hitting a rock that eventually resulted in engine failure. The remaining team members retired with a variety of mechanical problems.

Following the Rally of 1000 Lakes, Ford had accumulated enough points to give them a six point lead over Fiat in the World Championship. The next championship round was in Canada, when on 14th September the Critérium du Québec rally took place. Fiat made a determined effort by entering five cars, and for the first time the driver line-up included the German driver, Walter Röhrl partnered by Christian Geistdörfer. Three of the 131s retired with engine problems, but Salonen/Markkula and Lampinen/Sölve finished first and second, after the long time leader, Vatanen, retired his Ford Escort RS1800 with engine problems.

Moving on to its home ground on October 4, for the 'Rallye San Remo,' Fiat made a determined effort and entered six cars, three were driven by Fiat 'regulars,' Bacchelli, Röhrl and Verini, supplemented by Tony Fassina and Livio Lorenzelli. The sixth car was the Fiat France car, driven as usual by Andruet. The Fiat team was confronted by four Lancia Stratos, which ironically were prepared in the same workshop as the Fiats, and three works Ford Escort RS 1800s. In the main event, it certainly was Fiat's day, as it filled the first three places, led by Andruet and his new partner Christian Delferier, with Verini/Bruno Scabini second, and Fassina/Mauro Mannini third. The highest placed Stratos was fourth, and the highest placed Ford was fifth. This result put Fiat ahead of Ford in the World Championship ranking.

The next championship round was the Tour de Corse in Corsica, starting on November 5. As usual, strong competition was expected from two works Ford Escorts and four Lancia

An early 'Olio Fiat' liveried 131 Abarth Rally at an unknown event during 1976/77. (Courtesy FCA)

Right: Verini/Rossetti finished in fifth place in the 1977 Rally of Portugal. (Courtesy GR)

Left: Lampinen/Sölve finish in second place in the Critérium du Québec. (Courtesy GR)

Bottom left: The Critérium du Québec was unlucky for Alén/Kivimaki. (Courtesy GR)

Stratos, so Fiat responded by sending three cars for Bernard Darniche/Alain Mahé, Bacchelli/Scabini and Verini/Russo; these were supplemented by three cars entered by Fiat France. The French team consisted of Andruet, Francis Vincent/Calvier Vincent and an all-female entry for Michèle Mouton/Francoise Conconi. However in the actual event, both Fords retired and only two Stratos finished, one in second place with the other in fourth place. Therefore, Fiat finished in first, third and fifth places, led by Darniche, then Bacchelli and Vincent.

Thus, although there was still one more round to take place, Fiat became the 1977 World Rally Championship for Manufacturers. One can only imagine the celebrations that took place and also the relief that management's decision to concentrate on Fiat, as distinct from Lancia, had been vindicated, as had the significant investment of resources. Although an official World Championship for Drivers was not introduced until 1979, for 1977 and 1978, the FIA Cup for Drivers was introduced. The 1977 Cup winner was Sandro Munari, who had been Lancia's star driver of the Stratos.

Despite the fact that the World Championship for Manufacturers was now held by Fiat, it did enter a team for the final championship round of the year. The event was the RAC Rally held in Britain between 20-24 November. Three official works cars were sent, and were supplemented by three more cars entered by Graham Warner's Chequered Flag team. It was widely assumed that the Fiat 131s could not match the pace of the Team Ford Escort RS1800s. So it proved to be, with Lampinen/Sölve the highest placed Fiat in seventh position. Timo Mäkinen/Henry Lidden eventually finished in 11th place, with the other four cars all retiring for various reasons. The winning Ford Escort RS1800 was driven by Waldegård, and Englishman Russell Brookes was third in his similar car. Thus, despite the 'high' of winning the World Championship, the year ended on a definite 'low' for Fiat.

In order to further enhance its chances of repeating the World Championship success of

Andruet/Delferier retired with a broken halfshaft in the 1977 Acropolis Rally. (Courtesy GR)

1977, for 1978 Fiat decided to 'retire' the Lancia Stratos team and concentrate its efforts on the 131s, thus providing the latter with better prospects. So the team entered the first event, seemingly better prepared than ever with its highly talented list of drivers and navigators.

The first 1978 championship event was, as usual, the Monte Carlo Rally which took place between January 21-28. With the starters exceeding 200, including the four Fiat team cars, there was a wide variety of competitors in many different types of car; it did appear nevertheless that Fiat would dominate. In the end things didn't go according to plan, as the winner was a privately entered Porsche 911 driven by Jean-Pierre Nicholas and, amazingly, two Renault 5 Alpines finished second and third. All the Fiats finished, with the highest placed fourth, driven by Röhrl/Geistdörfer, and the remainder finished in fifth, sixth and eighth places. The relatively poor performance of the Fiats was in part due to Verini spinning his 131 in between snow banks on the Col de Perty stage and becoming stuck, not only causing him to lose time, but also the rest of the team who were all behind him!

The next round of the manufacturers' championship took place in Sweden from February 10-12. Team Fiat entered three cars, to be driven by Alén, Lampinen and Salonen, but for the first time this year they faced Team Ford Escort RS1800s. In the event, Waldegård driving an Escort RS1800, won from teammate Mikkola. Alén/Kivimaki finished third in their Fiat 131, while of the other Fiats, the car driven by Lampinen finished sixth and that of Salonen retired. Once again the Fords had demonstrated the benefit of their superior power and lower weight.

From Sweden the action moved south to Africa for the Safari Rally, but, as previously, Fiat chose not to make the journey, as it was felt the 131 was not capable of withstanding the physical punishment it would suffer on the many unmade roads used. The eventual result saw the first three places taken by Peugeot, Porsche (surprisingly), and Datsun, none of which would have any significant impact on the manufacturers' championship. Due to the surprise victory in the Monte Carlo Rally earlier, plus this result and some later useful placings, Porsche eventually finished fourth in the manufacturers' championship.

Better results were anticipated for the Fiat Team at the Rallye de Portugal held on April 19-23. Three Fiats were entered for Alén, Röhrl and, for the first time, Sandro Munari, partnered by Piero Sodano. It was clearly going to be a fiercely fought contest, for in addition to the four-car Ford Team, there was also stiff competition from Toyota, Vauxhall and a solitary Lancia Stratos. It proved to be an exceedingly tough event with the lead changing frequently between the Fiats and Fords. Two Fords retired with broken half-shafts, one Fiat suffered broken wheel studs and another a disintegrated clutch. These incidents left Alén battling with Mikkola's Ford, until the latter car hit a rock and was delayed while a tyre was replaced. Thus Alén won, followed by the Escorts of Mikkola and Nicolas.

The next manufacturers' championship round took place in Greece from May 29 to June 2 at the Acropolis Rally. Fiat entered the usual team of three cars, for Alén, Röhrl and Munari. Fortunately for the Italian team, on this occasion there were no official Ford entries and so most of the opposition came from Datsun, Toyota, Opel and numerous other 'also rans.' In the end the Fiats achieved a noteworthy first and second place finish, with the Datsun of Shekhar Mehta in third place. Röhrl was the winner followed by Alén, however the third Fiat entry of Munari retired.

There was then an almost three month wait for the next event, which was the 1000 Lakes Rally held in Finland on August 25-27. The Fiat works entry was two cars to be driven by Alén and Salonen, it also supplied two older models for the Finnish Fiat agent, to be driven by Lampinen and Hannu Valtaharju. Despite Ford's confidence of victory, it was not to be, as unreliability sidelined two of its cars and the highest placed attained was eighth. Fiat scored a one-two victory led by Alén and Salonen, with Lampinen's Finnish Fiat entered car finishing fifth. The other Finnish Fiat entered car retired. Salonen second place was achieved despite his rolling the car at one point! Fiat now had a comfortable lead over Ford in the manufacturers' championship.

Two weeks later, the Critérium du Québec took place in Canada and Fiat fielded three cars to be driven by Röhrl, Alén and Salonen. Ford chose not to enter, so the Fiats had little serious opposition to contend with, and, as

WALTER RÖHRL

Born in Regensburg, Germany, on March 7, 1947, Walter Röhrl was the youngest son of a stonemason. On leaving school he became a qualified ski instructor and an enthusiastic motorist. He was also employed as a chauffeur to the commercial director of his employers, covering large mileages annually.

Due in part to his active involvement in sport, in 1968 he was given the opportunity to take part in a rally, and by 1973 was entered in World Rally Championship events by Opel. His first championship victory came in 1975 when he won that year's Acropolis Rally in Greece. In 1978 he joined Fiat as part of its Fiat 131 Abarth Rally based team. Up until then, Walter had not been consistently successful, but that was about to change! The first victory for his new team came in 1978 when he once again won the Acropolis Rally. This was followed by six further victories over the period 1978 to 1981. In 1980 he became World Rally Champion, a feat that he repeated in 1982, when he was driving for Opel. At the time of his first championship win for drivers he was the youngest champion at 33 years of age, although Markku Alén, the next champion, was 29 in 1981.

Having fallen out with Opel due to his dislike of the RAC Rally and the promotion of Rothmans (he was a non-smoker), he joined Lancia in 1983 to drive the new Lancia Rally 037. He won three times in the Lancia, helping the team secure the World Championship for Manufacturers in 1983. 1984 saw Walter join Audi to drive the four-wheel drive Quattro. Over the next four years he scored two more wins and several podium positions. On his retirement from front line rallying he continued to take part in a variety of events, one of which was the Pike's Peak hillclimb in the USA, which he won in 1987 driving an Audi Quattro. In 1992 he took part in the 24-hour race at the Nürburgring in his home country, Germany. He eventually became a test driver for Porsche.

Walter Röhrl was notable for the cool and effective manner in which he drove, and was considered by many to be the best-ever rally driver. He won the Monte Carlo Rally four times in succession, driving a different make of car in each event, a feat that has never been repeated. He won 14 World Championship rallies and, from the start of his career with Fiat, was always accompanied by Christian Geistdörfer as his co-driver.

Alén/Kivimaki win in Portugal in 1978. (Courtesy GR)

San Remo 1978 – Munari/Mannucci soon to retire due to an accident. (Courtesy GR)

a consequence, led all the stages. In the end Röhrl won from Alén, and Salonen retired with a broken differential. In third place came Anders Kulläng in an Opel Kadet GTE, partnered with Bruno Bergland.

The next championship round was closer to home for the Italian teams: the San Remo rally held on 3-7 October. Fiat entered three cars, to be driven by Röhrl, Munari and Verini, but, as there were no Ford works entries due to a strike, the main opposition came from Lancia Stratos. For his first time, Alén was driving a works Stratos. There was also serious opposition from several privately entered Porsche 911s. Initially the Fiats of Röhrl and Munari both led on several sections until they both retired due to accidents, allowing Alén to take the lead, which he held until the finish. The one remaining works Fiat, driven by Verini, finished second, ahead of a Porsche 911 driven by Vincent. In addition to the manufacturers' championship, the FIA Cup for Drivers had been taking place at a number of events during the year, and the San Remo result confirmed Markku Alén as the 1978 Cup winner. From 1979 onwards the Cup became the World Drivers' Championship.

However, in terms of the manufacturers' championship for 1978 there were still three more rounds to take place and, theoretically, Ford could still take the championship, although the current industrial problems it was experiencing made this unlikely. The next round was the Rallye Côte d'Ivoire (Ivory Coast Rally) and Fiat decided not to enter a works team, but supplied a car for Frenchman Jean Vinatier to drive. Vinatier was then managing the Fiat France team, however the gesture was pointless in the end, as Vinatier crashed and was eliminated. Jean-Pierre Nicolas was the eventual winner in his Peugeot 504.

Fiat entered with a full team for the next

Röhrl/Geistdörfer at night on the 1978 RAC Rally, they finished sixth – note the co-driver in the middle of the back seat, soon to be disallowed. (Courtesy GR)

round, the Tour de Corse in Corsica which took place on November 4-5. The Fiat entries comprised two official team cars for Darniche and Munari, and two Fiat France cars for Andruet and Mouton; the main opposition came from two Lancia Stratos. In the event, the Stratos challenge faded away as both cars retired, leaving the Team Fiat cars a clear run to the finish. At the finish it was Darniche first, Andruet second, and Munari third, with the fourth car in fifth place. Thus Fiat became the 1978 World Champion manufacturer.

What a year it had been for the Italian team, not only was it once again World Champion manufacturer, but also had a member of the team, Markku Alén, who was the winner of the FIA Cup for drivers. Alén had driven both Fiat 131s and Lancia Stratos during the year.

Fiat decided to send a single car to the RAC Rally held on November 19-23. The driver of the Fiat was Röhrl, but in addition two Lancia Stratos were also entered to be driven by Alén and Munari. The event was dominated by Ford Escort RS1800s; both Lancias retired, but Röhrl managed to finish a disappointing sixth.

At the start of 1979, most observers were confident that the year would see a close battle between Fiat and Ford, and, bearing in mind that the former had been World Champion manufacturer for the previous two years, it was the clear favourite. How wrong can you be, as will become clear from the results! The season started as usual in January, with the Monte Carlo Rally, an event that the Fiat 131s had never won. This year was no exception as Darniche in a Lancia Stratos won from Waldegård in a Ford Escort RS1800; in fact Waldegård was the moral winner as his car was delayed by large rocks that had been deliberately placed in his path and caused a 40-second delay, yet he still finished only six seconds behind the winner. The best of the four Fiats entered, driven by Alén, managed to finish third behind Darniche and Waldegård. Of the remaining three Fiats, Andruet was fourth and Mouton seventh, but Röhrl retired with engine problems towards the end. What was now clear was the fact that the Fiat 131s lacked power when compared to the latest Ford Escort RS 1800s. It also seemed clear that, whilst the Fords had improved significantly, the Fiats hadn't.

The next championship round was the Swedish Rally and for some reason, not known, only a single Fiat was entered for Alén to drive. Whilst Alén's performance was good enough to gain him third place, it was once again clear that the Fiats could not match the pace of the Fords and, in this event, the Saab 99 Turbo. Stig Blomqvist, partnered by Björn Cederburg, won with Waldegård second in his Ford. The Rallye de Portugal was the next championship round, and Fiat had decided not to participate, despite having won in 1978, and so the Rally turned into a Ford benefit with Mikkola and Waldegård finishing first and second respectively.

Apparently Fiat's decision not to compete in Portugal was down to the fact that it was making a determined effort for the next event, the Safari Rally. The Safari Rally was renowned for its tough nature, unmade roads and variable weather conditions, both of which could cause havoc with suspension systems. Fiat built three brand new 'heavyweight' cars for this event to be driven by Alén, Röhrl and Munari. There were also two privately entered cars. Nobody had seriously expected the Fiats to win, and in the end they didn't, but amazingly all those entered completed the event. Alén drove superbly to finish third behind the Datsun 160J of Shekhar Mehta/Mike Doughty and the large Mercedes 450SLC of Mikkola/Arne Herz. The Fiats put on a remarkable display of reliability in that all five finished. Röhrl came in eighth, despite an accident with a non-competing vehicle and suffering a broken windscreen due to colliding with a bird; Munari was tenth. The two privately entered cars also finished although lower down the final ranking.

The action then moved to Greece for the Acropolis Rally held during May, and then over to the Antipodes in July for the New Zealand Rally. Fiat chose not to enter any official team cars for these events. In the Acropolis Rally there were several Fiat 127s and 128s, but none finished, and in New Zealand a privately entered 131 finished in eleventh place. Apparently Fiat had hoped that a sole Lancia Stratos, driven by Darniche, in Greece, might have kept the Fords in check, but it was not to be as the car retired. Waldegård won in Greece and Mikkola in New

Röhrl and Daniele Audetto at the 1978 Burmah Rally, Röhrl finished in fourth place. (Courtesy GR)

Zealand, both driving Ford Escort RS1800s. In fact, in New Zealand the Fords filled the first three places.

Fiat entered just one works car for the 1000 Lakes Rally in Finland, held on August 24-28. The works entry, driven by Alén, was supported by two 131's entered by the local Fiat agent; these were to be driven by Henri Toivonen/Juha Paajanen and Ulf Grönholm/Bob Rehnström. Alén, having battled with the Ford Escorts of Vatanen and Mikkola, took victory after a magnificent drive; this was his third win out of four attempts. Vatanen was second and Waldegård third. Of the two locally entered Fiats, Grönholm finished fourth and Toivonen retired. So at last Fiat had a long awaited victory, although the World Championship for Manufacturers was now beyond its reach.

The next round of the World Championship was the Critérium du Québec in Canada, but, once again, Fiat decided not to enter thus leaving the event in the hands of Ford. This duly happened with Waldegård winning and his team-mate Vatanen finishing third. Splitting the Ford pair

Engine failure ruined Röhrl's 1979 Monte Carlo Rally. (Courtesy GR)

Rallying: Fiat Returns

Röhrl/Geistdörfer came second in the 1979 San Remo Rally. (Courtesy GR)

Another picture of Röhrl in the 1979 San Remo Rally. (Courtesy FF)

Whether it was because the 1979 World Championship for Manufacturers was now beyond its reach or some other reason is not clear, but Fiat chose not to enter the 'Tour de Corse' and left it to Fiat France to uphold its reputation. Likewise there were no works Ford entries. In the actual event, Darniche, driving a Lancia Stratos won from Renault Alpine and a Porsche 911. Of the two Fiat France entered Fiats, that driven by Mouton finished in fifth place, whilst the other, driven by Andruet, retired.

The penultimate round of the 1979 World Championship was the RAC Rally, held as usual in November; this year there were 12 rounds in total. Fiat entered just one 131 for Röhrl and was persuaded to enter a Lancia Stratos for Alén. As was becoming the norm, the rally turned into a Ford benefit with Mikkola beating teammate Russell Brookes, who was partnered by Paul White, both in Escort RS1800s. Fords also finished fourth and sixth. Of the Fiat supported entries, Alén finished fifth in his Stratos and Röhrl eighth in his 131. Once again it was clear the Fiat 131s could not match the pace of the Ford Escort RS1800s. Earlier in the year Fiat had entered one car in the Circuit of Ireland Rally, to be driven by Salonen/Seppo Harjanne. Salonen retired having had a spectacular accident which resulted in his car overturning, but thankfully no-one was hurt.

The World Championship for Manufacturers had already been decided in Ford's favour, so neither Ford nor Fiat contested the final round on the Ivory Coast in December. This turned out to be a Mercedes benefit with its 450SLC models filling the first four places. 1979 hadn't been a good year for Fiat, when it eventually finished third in the manufacturers championship, behind Ford and Datsun. In terms of the newly instigated World Drivers' Championship, it was the Ford team mates, Björn Waldegård and Hannu Mikkola who finished first and second respectively. Fiat had only won one event, the 1000 Lakes Rally in Finland, during the year, which was very disappointing when compared to 1978, with five outright wins. However, the Fiat team's morale must have been raised when it learnt that its most competitive opponent, Ford, with its Escort RS1800s, was going to be missing during 1980 while it developed a new car. The driver line up also changed as Sandro Munari left, but there was no shortage of drivers available.

was Salonen in his Datsun 160J. It was Ford who chose not to enter the next round at San Remo, and the main beneficiary was Fassina in a Jolly Club entered Lancia Stratos, but there was some consolation for Fiat, as Röhrl and Attilio Betega, who was partnered by Maurizio Perissinot, were second and third respectively and the remaining works entry, driven by Alén, was sixth.

Not a good day at the office! Salonen's car leaves the road in spectacular fashion at the 1979 Circuit of Ireland. (Courtesy GR)

As usual the first round of the World Championship was the Monte Carlo Rally, held as normal at the end of January. Fiat entered no fewer than five 131s, one front-wheel drive 'Ritmo' as an experiment, and there was also a privately entered Lancia Stratos. In the event, which was run under better weather conditions than normal as there was little snow and ice, Röhrl led for much of the time. His main challenger was Darniche in the elderly Stratos, despite Darniche suffering from a bout of flu. So it finished with third place being taken by Waldegård, the Ritmo finished a surprising sixth driven by Attilio Bettega, partnered by Mario Mannucci, and in seventh place was Mouton in a Fiat France car. The experiment with the Ritmo was obviously not considered successful and the car was not seen again as a works entry. Mouton's team-mate Andruet retired, as did the other works car of Alén. This was Fiat's first victory in the Monte Carlo Rally with the 131 model, although the Fiat backed Lancia Stratos had won on no fewer than four occasions. Thus, 1980 had started well for the Fiat team.

The action now moved to Scandinavia for the Swedish Rally, which took place from February 15-17. Surprisingly, the Fiat 131 proved no match for an Opel Ascona driven by Anders Kulläng and Bruno Berglund, or the Saab 99 Turbo of Stig Blomqvist and Björn Cederburg. The best Waldegård could achieve was third place behind these two.

Then came the Rallye du Portugal on March

4-9. Fiat entered three cars for Röhrl, Alén and Bettega. Although Darniche, driving his elderly Lancia Stratos, actually led in the early stages until engine failure caused his retirement, it was fairly straightforward for the Fiat team. Röhrl had a trouble free run to victory, while team-mate Alén finally finished second after a troublesome drive. The third 131, driven by Bettega, was involved in a road accident which caused his early retirement. Röhrl had now established a lead in the Drivers' Championship, which he kept until the end of the season.

Fiat gave the 1980 Safari Rally a miss this year, and so the next Championship round was the Acropolis Rally in Greece. Although there were no works Ford Escorts entered, there were two Rothmans team Escorts that, unfortunately for the Fiat contingent, proved to be as quick as the works cars. Whilst one Rothmans car retired, the other, driven by Vatanen, won convincingly from the Datsun 160J of Salonen. The best placed Fiat was that of Alén who finished in third place. It was a small consolation for the Fiat team that all its cars finished, Röhrl took fifth place after a troublesome drive in a car that he felt wasn't handling properly, and Bettega finished in eighth place having suffered various problems en route. The sole Lancia Stratos of Darniche retired in the early stages of the event.

An innovation for this year's championship was a round in South America, in Argentina. Based in the Tucumán Province, the Rally Codasur took place on 19-24 July. In addition to its usual three drivers, Fiat achieved a significant coup by hiring Argentinian Formula 1 hero, Carlos Reutemann, to drive for them. In addition to his 'hero' standing, he also brought with him generous sponsorship that helped defray Fiat's significant expense in travelling to Argentina. The main competition came from the Datsun 160Js and Mercedes-Benz with its mighty 500SLC cars.

However, it was widely anticipated that Fiat would win, and that is what happened. Röhrl, having led from start to finish, won from Mikkola in one of the huge Mercedes-Benz 500 SLC, while Reutemann justified his inclusion in the Fiat team by finishing third, accompanied by Mirko Perissutti. Both Alén and Bettega retired with engine problems due to oil loss when sumps were cracked on hard landings. Next it was back to Scandinavia for the 1000 Lakes Rally held on 29-31 August. There was only one Fiat 131 entered, and that was by Autonovo (The Fiat Finnish Agent) for three times winner, Alén, to drive. In addition Autonovo also entered a Fiat Ritmo for a local driver. In the event, Alén led from start to finish, thus securing his fourth victory in this event over five years. Alén was pursued throughout by Vatanen driving a Team Rothmans Escort RS1800. Per Eklund and Hans Sylvan finished third in their Triumph TR7 V8. The Autonovo entered Fiat Ritmo failed to finish.

Following the Rally Codasur in Argentina, Fiat had flown one car direct to New Zealand in readiness for that country's rally in September. Preparation was carried out in New Zealand and the car allocated to Röhrl to drive. It was a three-way contest between the Fiat, the Datsun of Salonen and the Ford Escort of Pentti Airikkala and Chris Porter. Salonen led for most of the event, finishing ahead of Röhrl. Airikkola had a serious accident which caused his retirement and a spell in hospital. Third place then went to Mikkola in one of the mighty Mercedes-Benz 500 SLCs.

Then it was closer to home for the Rallye San Remo in October. However, significant logistical difficulties arose for Fiat due to industrial action at the factory that prevented access. Luckily for Fiat, it was able to borrow cars from various private teams that were unaffected by the strikes. This meant that Röhrl would be driving a Jolly Club car, Alén a car from the Quattro Rombi team, and Bettega a car from the River Team Racing Équipe. The main competition was considered to be from the Team Rothmans Fords, and so it proved. A measure of how closely fought the rally was, is that no fewer than five different drivers led at various times and, even more surprising, nine different drivers set fastest times in the various stages. In the end, however, Fiat 'came good' with Röhrl winning in the Jolly Club car, but a reflection of the intense competition was the fact that Team Rothmans Escorts came second and third, driven by Vatanen and Mikkola. Bettega brought his Fiat home into sixth place, while Alén retired the third car. The Jolly Club had entered another Fiat 131, but that failed to finish.

For the Rallye de France held on the island of Corsica at the end of October, Fiat mounted a serious challenge. Having come to an agreement with the trade unions, it was able to enter factory-prepared cars for Röhrl, Bettega and Darniche, Alén now having switched his allegiance to Lancia. The three works cars were supported by two Fiat France cars for Andruet and Mouton, the latter being partnered by

Bettega/Bernaccini had a road accident that eliminated them from the 1980 Portugese Rally. (Courtesy FCA)

In the 1980 Acropolis Rally, Röhrl/Geistdörfer could only manage fifth place after handling problems delayed them. (Courtesy GR)

Annie Arrii for this event. There were no Team Rothmans Ford Escorts entered in this event and the main competition came from Porsche 911s and Datsun 160Js. In the actual event it was the Porsches that mounted the strongest challenge with Jean-Luc Therier, partnered by Michel Vial, finishing first, and his team-mate Alain Coppier and Josépha Laloz finishing third. Consolation came for both Fiat and Röhrl due to him finishing second and clinching that year's World Championship for Manufacturers and World Rally Champion. Röhrl's championship win was by the substantial margin of 54 points over his nearest rival, Hannu Mikkola.

No doubt due to the fact that Fiat had won both the manufacturers' championship and the drivers' championship, no works Fiats were entered in the two final events of the 1980 season. The RAC Rally was won by Henri Toivonen driving a Talbot Sunbeam Lotus and the Ivory Coast Rally was won by Waldegård in a Mercedes-Benz 500 SLC, however in the latter event there was a single Fiat 131 driven by Munari that finished in sixth place.

For 1981, Fiat made it clear that there would not be sufficient funding to mount a full-scale championship challenge and there was no replacement in sight. As a result Walter Röhrl decided to leave, but Markku Alén decided to stay after much deliberation. Fiat also realised that the appearance of the four-wheel drive Audi Quattro was likely to have a major impact, as did the Lancia Stratos when it appeared in 1973, and that development of the 131 Fiat Abarth Rally had reached its maximum potential. Therefore, whilst the works 131s did appear at several championship events, the Fiat-Lancia team focused its attention on developing a new car, which eventually turned out to be another World Championship car, the Fiat-Lancia 037.

Fiat entered the first championship event of the year, the Monte Carlo Rally, with just two cars. One was for Alén and the other for newcomer Dario Cerrato, who was partnered by Luciano Guizzardi. Despite the Audi challenge failing to materialise, as both cars retired, it wasn't a good day for the Fiat team, Alén eventually finishing in seventh place, having struggled with a lack of grip on the ice and snow covered roads. Cerrato struggled home in 11th place, most likely encountering the same difficulties as Alén. Fiat didn't enter the Swedish Rally, presumably because similar snow and ice conditions as at the Monte Carlo Rally were anticipated. That event saw the first championship victory for the new Audi Quattro driven by Mikkola.

The Rallye de Portugal was the next championship round and Fiat entered three cars, to be driven by Alén, Bettega and Cerrato. Although the 131 was now clearly past its best, the fact that they had won this event in 1977, 1978 and 1980 must have given rise to a degree of optimism. If so, it was justified because Alén won, beating Toivonen's Talbot Sunbeam Lotus and Waldegård's Toyota Celica, who were second and third respectively. The other team cars failed to finish, Bettega with engine problems and Cerrato with suspension failure. This victory was to be the last one for a 131 in a World Championship event.

Fiat decided not to enter the Safari Rally in Africa or the Tour de Corse in Corsica. So it was June when the works 131s next appeared. This was for the Acropolis Rally in Greece and Fiat entered two cars for Alén and Bettega; these were basically re-bodied 1979 cars! Controversy reared its head again when the works Audi Quattros were disqualified on technical infringements (shades of Monte Carlo here!) and so the main competition came from the Ford Escorts of Team Rothmans, which, similar to Fiat, had entered two cars. Of the two Team Rothmans cars, one retired, but the other, driven by Vatanen, won. Both Fiats finished strongly in second and third places, with Alén finishing ahead of his team-mate Bettega.

The next appearance of the works 131s was nearly three months later for the 1000 Lakes Rally in Finland. As he had won the last four out of five of these events, Alén was the sole Fiat entry and was considered to be a very strong competitor. Unfortunately, Alén suffered a high speed roll and the subsequent electrical faults were probably a consequence of that incident, nevertheless he managed to finish an amazing second by a mere 59 seconds behind the winner, Vatanen in a Ford Escort. Early leader Mikkola in his Audi Quattro lost time when his engine required attention, dropping him back to third place.

The San Remo Rally was the last time that the works Fiat 131 Abarth Rally cars would be seen. As a swansong, a team of four cars was entered to be driven by Alén, Bettega, Cerrato and newcomer Adartico Vudafieri, partnered by Arnaldo Bernacchini. Sadly, it wasn't to be the glorious finale to the 131's rallying career that Fiat had presumably hoped for. The event was dominated by the Audi Quattros with Mouton winning, but Toivonen's Talbot Sunbeam Lotus took second place and Fassina's Opel Ascona finished third. Of the Fiats, that of Bettega and Vudafieri retired, and of the other two Cerrato finished eighth, and Alén an unhappy ninth after suffering gearbox problems.

At lower levels Fiat 131 Abarths scored many wins, and in 1981 Adartico Vudafieri became European Rally Champion by a significant margin. With three Manufacturers' World Championships under its belt, Fiat had every justification for feeling satisfied that the time and effort, not to mention the cost, involved had been well repaid. As Fiat had now taken the decision that the Lancia brand, which of course it owned, would from then onwards be its sporting brand, it seemed that the name 'Fiat' would never again feature in world rallying, other than by private entrants. However, arising from its ownership of Abarth, in 2006 Fiat management decided that the new Abarth Grande Punto S2000 should be entered in World Championship events, and it certainly made an impact. At the end of that year, the Fiat Abarth Grande Punto S2000 was European Rally Champion, as well as winner of the International Rally Challenge (IRC) and the South-Western European Cup. It repeated the latter two results the following year. Also, in 2009, 2010 and 2011 Fiat Abarth Grande Puntos were European Rally Champions again. The cars were clearly labelled as Fiats, so the Fiat badge was once again seen on the international rally scene.

Second place for Alén/Kivimaki in the 1981 Acropolis Rally. (Courtesy GR)

Abarth Grande Punto IRC – 2006 European Rally Champion. (Courtesy FCA)

CHAPTER NINE
The Abarth Connection

Karl Abarth was born in Vienna in Austria in 1908 and, after an early career designing and racing motorcycles, he eventually moved to Italy on a permanent basis. His racing career finished after a serious accident, but he continued working as an engineer. At some point in time he became naturalised as an Italian citizen and changed his first name to Carlo. Through his work he got to know Ferdinand Porsche, Tazio Nuvolari, Piero Dusio and engineer Rudolph Hruska. Together they formed Cisitalia, which eventually collapsed and Dusio emigrated to Argentina. Carlo Abarth then, in 1949, established the firm that bears his name, Abarth & C, utilising his astrological sign, the scorpion, as the company badge.

Initially, Abarth concentrated on Fiat-engined cars, usually using the 1100cc engine. Also, when Cisitalia went into liquidation, in addition to a number of racing cars, Abarth found a special exhaust designed by former Cisitalia engineer Giovanni Savonuzzi. This is how the now legendary Abarth silencers came about. In 1950 the first Cisitalia-Abarth appears, although modified versions of the original Cisitalia cars, they now carried the Abarth Scorpion badge. It was in one of these cars in April 1950 that the great Tazio Nuvolari competed in his last motor race, which was the Monte Pellegrino-Palermo hillclimb. He won the 1100 class and finished fifth overall. This success was the start of the true Abarth story. Meanwhile Abarth concentrated on making sporting coupés and open models.

1955 saw the introduction of the 'Abarth 750 Derivative' based on the Fiat 600, which,

An Abarth 1000 Corsa model of 1965/67. (Courtesy FCA)

Abarth 850TCs on the race track. (Courtesy FCA)

An Abarth at an historic race event at Oulton Park.

An Abarth 750 coupé at the 1961 Le Mans race. (Courtesy NMM)

as recalled in Chapter five, made an auspicious debut in the 1956 Mille Miglia. Several developments followed, eventually culminating in the 1000 Corsa model of the mid-1950s. These were soon to be seen on race tracks everywhere. Abarths of all types were competing in different categories around the world, from inception until 1971 when Fiat took over. However, since then and, due to the fact that Abarth manages the Fiat competition department, its name still appears on competition models, albeit in conjunction with the latter.

1956 also saw Abarth enter into the world of record breaking. Utilising the Fiat 600-derived engine and an aerodynamic body created by Carrozzeria Nuccio Bertone and his designer Franco Scaglione, on 17-18 June, the first Abarth record car established a new 24-hour record for class H cars (501 to 750cc). Not satisfied with just one record, the same car went on to break many more records, now repainted in plain silver (originally it was red and white) and using 500cc and 800cc engines all based upon Fiat 600 engines. In total some

An Abarth at the Mont Ventoux Hillclimb. (Courtesy NMM)

20 records were established in the three classes involved.

The next record car appeared in 1957 and was designed by Pinin Farina, but powered by an Alfa Romeo Giuletta engine. It broke several records but, due to some irritation at Fiat over the use of Alfa Romeo engines (Fiat at that time did not own Alfa Romeo), the next series of record cars up until the mid 1960s were all Fiat powered. As a result, Pinin Farina built a second car, similar to the first, but this time powered by a Fiat 600 engine that was enlarged to 750cc. Between July 1957 and October 1958 this car set no fewer than 23 international records.

The new Fiat 500 was announced in 1957 and was viewed with sceptism over its small two-cylinder engine. Utilising a standard body, but modified engine, an Abarth-prepared 500 set six new records in February 1958, and, as a result, built a special record-breaking car with a streamlined body designed by Pinin Farina. This

Arturio Mezario at the 1971 Daytona 24-hour race. (Courtesy NMM)

Bertone-designed record-breaker on display, plus 8V. (Courtesy GR)

500 record car by Bertone at Monza. (Courtesy FCA)

purpose-built 500 set an amazing total of 28 records, the most established by any Fiat Abarth model. Apparently, Abarth built and tested all the Fiat 2300 S Coupés for the manufacturer and in 1963 took one of these large coupés to Monza for long distance record attempts. After five days, records were set for 5000 miles, 48 hours, 10,000km and 72 hours, but, due to a stone damaging the sump on the fifth day, the attempt was aborted before the five day record was achieved. In 1965 the OT Coupé and Spider were launched (OT stands for Omologata Turismo, or homologated for touring) and during October of that year 1450cc and 2000cc versions established more records. The last record attempts took place during October 1966 when a new Formula 2 car fitted with a 2000cc engine set several new records. Abarth never again attempted to set new records.

Another manufacturer now features in the Abarth story: Autobianchi. Created in 1955 as a joint venture between Banchi, Fiat and Pirelli, Autobianchi only produced a limited range of small cars over its lifetime. The Autobianchi project came about due to Bianchi's declining sales of motor cars and motor cycles, the latter being what the firm was best known for. All the cars were based upon Fiat mechanicals, initially the 500. In 1971 the most significant Autobianchi was introduced, the A112. With Fiat now owning both Abarth and Autobianchi, development of the A112 into a competition car was undertaken by Abarth and resulted in the Abarth A112. In the 1976 Monte Carlo Rally, 14 A112s started and only two failed to finish and the highest placed car narrowly missed winning its class.

In 1971, Carlo Abarth sold his company to Fiat. Fiat decided that it did not want the racing division and sold it to Enzo Osella, thus ending Abarth's direct involvement in motor racing and hillclimbing. Osella, amongst the cars, spares and technicians, also inherited Arturo Merzzario, the racing driver who had been associated with Abarth for a number of years. In due course, Osella set up its own racing team. Although Fiat no longer participated directly in motor racing, it nevertheless established a racing department headed by engine designer Aurelio Lampredi, the famous former Ferrari engineer. The Fiat Group's racing department was placed under the auspices of Abarth.

The first product of the 'new' Abarth was the Abarth 124 Spider Rally, based upon the Fiat 124 that had first appeared in 1964. As recalled in Chapter eight, the Abarth 124 Spider Rally brought the Fiat name, in combination with Abarth, back into the forefront of world motorsport after many years absence. On four consecutive years the 124 finished second in the World Rally Championship for Manufacturers and, in the latter two instances, to Lancia, who

Pininfarina 750 record breaker in workshop. (Courtesy FCA)

750 record-breaker on display at the 1957 Geneva Motor Show. (Courtesy FCA)

since 1969 had been a member of the 'Fiat family'. Over this period some five victories were achieved.

The next venture was the development of the Fiat X-1/9 for rallying, but this was short lived because Fiat management preferred the 131 Abarth project as it was thought to be more effective in terms of marketing. Again Chapter eight lists the impressive results achieved by the Abarth 131 Rally that resulted in three World Rally Championships for manufacturers. The record of the Abarth Grande Punto in winning several titles has also been covered in Chapter eight.

It was during 1970/71 that the Commissione Sportiva Automobilistica Italiana (the CSAI) suggested to Fiat that it should support the introduction of a new class of single-seat racing cars to encourage the development of young Italian racing drivers. Fiat was entrusted with the design and construction of these cars, which were to race under the title of 'Formula Italia'. This was one of the first, if not the first, such formulae based upon a single engine manufacturer. It led to the introduction of many other single make formulae such as Formula Ford, Formula Vee, Formula BMW, etc. As Abarth was now running the racing division of Fiat, it was entrusted with the design and construction of these cars which used the twin camshaft Fiat-Abarth 1600cc engine from the Fiat 124S. Some 150 cars were built for the formula, which ran until 1979, when it was replaced by 'Formula Fiat Abarth'. The success of the formula can be judged by the number of future Italian Grand Prix drivers who emerged, these included Michele Alboreto, Bruno Giacomelli, Riccardo Patrese and Piercarlo Ghinzani.

In 1979 'Formula Fiat Abarth' was

Range of Pininfarina designs on display. (Courtesy FCA)

Formula Fiat Abarth cars on display. (Courtesy FCA)

introduced and replaced Formula Italia. This class of racing was for single-seat racing cars of up to 2000cc. To contain costs and simplify matters as far as possible, many standard components from within the Fiat Group's range were utilised. The engine was the 1995cc unit from the Lancia Beta, and the suspension utilised parts from the Fiat 131. In a similar manner to the previous Formula Italia, the series was aimed at encouraging young Italian drivers, and produced many talented drivers such as future Grand Prix participants Emanuele Pirro, Alessandro Nannini and Dindo Capello.

Today Abarth lives on, its latest offering being the Abarth 500 which, as you would expect, is a high-performance version of the basic Fiat 500.

APPENDIX ONE
Technical Details

Key to Dimensions: a = wheelbase; b = length; c = width; d = height; e = weight

Year	Type	Engine	Power	Valves	Suspension	Wheels	Brakes	Steering	Dimensions
1900	6 HP Corsa	Rear 2-cyl 1082cc	6hp	Opposed vertical	Front rigid, elliptic springs Rear rigid Semi-elliptic springs	Wood	Foot – transmission Hand – rear wheels	Worm & helical	a: 5ft 8in b: 7ft 6in c: 4ft 5in d: 5ft 3in e: 2314lb
1902	8 HP	Front 2-cyl 1082cc	8hp	Overhead inlet Side exhaust	As 6 HP	As 6 HP	As 6 HP	As 6 HP	a: 5ft 6in b: 7ft 10in c: 4ft 5in d: 4ft 11in e: 1433lb
1902	12 HP Corsa	Front 4-cyl 3770cc	12hp	As 8 HP	Front & rear rigid semi-elliptic	As 6 HP	As 6 HP	As 6 HP	a: 7ft 0in b: 9ft 9in c: ? d: ? e: 1653lb
1902	24 HP Corsa	Front 4-cyl 6371cc	24hp	Side	As 12 HP	As 6 HP	Foot & hand transmission	As 6 HP	a: 7ft 10in b: 10ft 10in c: ? d: ? e: 1441lb
1903	60 HP Corsa	Front 4-cyl 10603cc	60hp	As 24 HP	As 12 HP	As 6 HP	As 24 HP	As 6 HP	a: 9ft 9in b: 11ft 3in c: ? d: ? e: 2425lb
1904	75 HP Corsa	Front 4-cyl 14112cc	75hp	Overhead	As 12 HP	As 6 HP	As 24 HP	As 6 HP	a: 9ft 5in b: 12ft 6in c: 5ft 7in d: 4ft 5in e: 2215lb
1905	100 HP Corsa	Front 4-cyl 16286cc	100hp	As 75 HP	As 12 HP	As 6 HP	As 24 HP	As 6 HP	a: 9ft 4in b: 12ft 5in c: 5ft 5in d: 4ft 5in e: 2204lb

Year	Type	Engine	Power	Valves	Suspension	Wheels	Brakes	Steering	Dimensions
1905	110 HP Gordon Bennett Corsa	Front 4-cyl 16286cc	110hp	As 75 HP	As 12 HP	As 6 HP	As 24 HP	As 6 HP	a: 9ft 4in b: 12ft 5in c: 5ft 5in d: 4ft 5in e: 2204lb
1907	28-40 HP Targa Florio	Front 4-cyl 7363cc	60hp	Side	As 12 HP	As 6 HP	As 24 HP	As 6 HP	a: 9ft 6in b: 13ft 1in c: 4ft 8in d: ? e: 2314lb
1907	Taunus Corsa	Front 4-cyl 8004cc	72hp	Overhead	As 12 HP	As 6 HP	As 24 HP	As 6 HP	a: 10ft 7in b: 14ft 7in c: 4ft 7in d: ? e: 2590lb
1907	130 HP Grand Prix de France Corsa	Front 4-cyl 16286cc	130hp	As Taunus	As 12 HP	As 6 HP	As 24 HP	As 6 HP	a: 9ft 4in b: 10ft 0in c: 5ft 9in d: 4ft 4in e: 2259lb
1908	SB 4 Corsa	Front 4-cyl 18146cc	175hp	As Taunus	As 12 HP	As 6 HP	As 24 HP	As 6 HP	a: 8ft 1in b: 11ft 8in c: 4ft 1in d: ? e: 2645lb
1908	S 61 Corsa	Front 4-cyl 10087cc	115hp	As Taunus	As 12 HP	As 6 HP	As 24 HP	As 6 HP	a: 10ft 3in b: 14ft 9in c: 4ft 7in d: ? e: 2799lb
1911	S 74 Corsa	Front 4-cyl 14137cc	290hp	As Taunus	As 12 HP	As 6 HP	As 24 HP	As 6 HP	a: 10ft 4in b: 14ft 9in c: 4ft 7in d: ? e: 3306lb
1911	S 76 300 HP Record	Front 4-cyl 28353cc	290hp	As Taunus	As 12 HP	Rudge-Whitworth	As 24 HP	As 6 HP	a: 9ft 0in b: 12ft 3in c: 4ft 3in d: ? e: 4188lb
1914	S57/14B Corsa	Front 4-cyl 4492cc	135hp	Overhead valves and camshaft	As 12 HP	As S76	Mechanical with servo	As 6 HP	a: 9ft 2in b: 12ft 3in c: 4ft 3in d: ? e: 2535lb
1916	S57A/14B Corsa	Front 4-cyl 4859cc	150hp	As S57/14B	As 12 HP	As S76	As S57/14B	As 6 HP	a: 9ft 2in b: 12ft 5in c: 4ft 3in d: ? e: 2579lb

Year	Type	Engine	Power	Valves	Suspension	Wheels	Brakes	Steering	Dimensions
1921	804-401	Front 4-cyl 2973cc	112hp	As S57/14B	As 12 HP	As S76	As S57/14B	As 6 HP	a: 9ft 0in b: 12ft 3in c: 4ft 7in d: ? e: 1785lb
1921	501S & SS	Front 4-cyl 1460cc	S: 26.5hp SS: 72hp	S: side valves SS: overhead valves with overhead camshafts	As 12 HP	Sankey	As S57/14B	As 6 HP	a: 8ft 8in b: 12ft 6in c: 4ft 1in d: ? e: 2660lb
1921	801-402 Corsa	Front 8-cyl 2973cc	120hp	Overhead valves with twin overhead camshafts	As 12 HP	Rudge Whitworth	As S57/14B	As 6 HP	a: 9ft 0in b: 15ft 3in c: 5ft 6in d: ? e: 2028lb
1921	803-403 Corsa	Front 4-cyl 1486cc	62.5hp	As 801	As 12 HP	As 801	As S57/14B	As 6 HP	a: 7ft 6in b: 11ft 2in c: 4ft 6in d: 3ft 10in e: 1212lb
1922	804-404	Front 6-cyl 1991cc	112hp	As 801	As 12 HP	As 801	As S57/14B	As 6 HP	a: 8ft 2in b: 12ft 7in c: 4ft 10in d: 3ft 6in e: 2017lb
1923	805-405	Front 8-cyl 1979cc s/charged	130hp – Wittig 150hp – Roots	As 801	As 12 HP	As 801	As S57/14B	As 6 HP	a: 8ft 8in b: 14ft 2in c: 5ft 7in d: 4ft 2in e: 1499lb
1923	'Mephistopheles'	Front 6-cyl 21706cc	320hp	As 801	As 12 HP	As 801	Rear wheels only	As 6 HP	a: 11ft 3in b: 16ft 9in c: 6ft 0in d: 4ft 7in e: 3924lb
1927	806 Corsa	Front-12-cyl 1484cc s/charged	187hp Roots s/c	Overhead valves with triple overhead camshafts	As 12 HP	As 801	As S57/14B	As 6 HP	a: 7ft 10in b: 11ft 11in c: 4ft 9in d: 3ft 5in e: 1543lb
1929	514 MM/CA * Note: larger figures relate to MM	Front 4-cyl 1438cc	37hp	Side valves	As 12 HP	As 801	As S57/14B	As 6 HP	a: 9ft 1in/ 8ft 4in* b: 12ft 2in/ 12ft 1in c: 4ft 9in d: ? e: 2391/2148lb

Technical Details

Year	Type	Engine	Power	Valves	Suspension	Wheels	Brakes	Steering	Dimensions
1932 1st series/ 1934 2nd series	MM 508 Balilla S/CS * Note: Larger figures relate to 2nd series	Front 4-cyl 995cc	30hp sv 36hp ohv S 46hp ohv CS	Side valves – 1st series Overhead valves – 2nd series	As 12 HP	Wire	Hydraulic on all four wheels	As 6 HP	a: 7ft 6in/ 7ft 8in* b: 10ft 3in/ 12ft 1in c: 4ft 7in d: 4ft 7in e: 1742/1808lb
1937	508C MM	Front 4-cyl 1089cc	42hp	Overhead valves	Front: independent with coil springs Rear: rigid with semi-elliptic springs	Disc	As 508	As 6 HP	a: 7ft 112 b: 13ft 8in c: 4ft 10in d: 4ft 4in e: 2325lb
1947	1100S	Front 4-cyl 1089cc	51hp	As 508C	As 508C	As 508C	As 508C	As 6 HP	a: 7ft 11in b: 12ft 10in c: 4ft 10in d: 4ft 5in e: 2259lb
1950	1100ES	Front 4-cyl 1089cc	51hp	As 508C	As 508C	As 508C	As 508C	As 6 HP	a: 7ft 11in b: 13ft 5in c: 5ft 1in d: 4ft 5in e: 2778lb
1952	8V (Otto Vu)	Front 8-cyl 1996cc	105hp 1st series 127hp 2nd series	As 508C	Coil springs all round	Rudge Whitworth	As 508	Worm & roller	a: 7ft 10in b: 13ft 3in c: 5ft 1in d: 4ft 2in e: 2506lb
1953	1100/103TV	Front 4-cyl 1089cc	53hp	As 508C	As 508C	Disc	As 508	Worm & sector	a: 7ft 8in b: 12ft 4in c: 4ft 9in d: 4ft 10in e: 2622lb
1969	124 Abarth Rally	Front 4-cyl 1969: 1608cc 1978: 1995cc	1969: 114hp 1978: 122hp	Overhead valves and twin overhead camshafts	Coil springs all round- independent at front Rigid axle at rear	As 1100	Hydraulic, discs all round	Worm & roller	a: 7ft 5in b: 13ft 4in c: 5ft 3in d: 4ft 1in e: 2064lb
1976	131 Abarth Rally	Front- 4-cyl 1995cc	230hp Final model	As 124	Coil springs & independent all round	As 1100	As 124	Rack & pinion	a: 8ft 1in b: 13ft 8in c: 5ft 8in d: 4ft 6in e: 2050lb

APPENDIX TWO
Competition Results

Year	Event	Result	Car	Driver(s)
1899	Padua-Bassano-Vicenza-Padua	1	Welleyes	V Lancia
1900	Vincenza-Padua	1	6 HP Corsa – 108cc	V. Lancia
1902	Giro D'Italia	1	8 HP – 1082cc	G Agnelli
1904	Brescia-Cremona-Brescia	1	75 HP Corsa – 14112cc	V Lancia
1905	Gordon Bennett Cup	2 & 3	100 HP Corsa – 16286cc	F Nazzaro, A Cagno
1906	Vanderbilt Cup	2	100 HP	V Lancia
	French Grand Prix	2	100 HP	F Nazzaro
1907	Vanderbilt Cup	2	130 HP – 16286cc	F Nazzaro
	Targa Florio	1 & 2	28/40 HP – 7363cc	F Nazzaro (1), V Lancia (2)
	French Grand Prix	1	130 HP	F Nazzaro
1908	Kaiserpreis	1	Taunus – 8004cc	F Nazzaro
	Targa Florio	2	SB 4 – 12045cc	V Lancia
	American Grand Prix	1	S 61- 10087cc	L Wagner
1909	Targa Bologna	1	SB 4	F Nazzaro
	Targa Florio	2	SB 4	V Florio
1911	Vanderbilt Cup	2	SB 4	E Parker
	Grand Prix de France	1	S 74 – 14137cc	V Hemery
1912	American Grand Prix	1	S 74	D Bruce-Brown
	French Grand Prix	2	S 74	L Wagner
	USA Grand Prix	1	S 74	C Bragg
1922	Indianapolis 500	2	S 74	E Tezlaff/C Bragg
	French Grand Prix	1	804-404 – 1991cc	F Nazzaro
	Italian Grand Prix	1 & 2	804-404	P Bordino, F Nazzaro
	Gran Premio Vetturette	1 & 2	803-403	P Bordino, E Giaccone
1923	Gran Premio Vetturette	1	803-403	A Cagno
	European Grand Prix	1& 2	805-405	C Salamano, F Nazzaro
1924	Alessandria circuit	1 & 2	?	U Massino, 'Nino'
1927	Milan Grand Prix	1	806 – 1484cc supercharged	P Bordino
1929	Monte Carlo Rally	1& 2	509	J Bignan
1948	Mille Miglia	2	1100S	A Comirato/L Com-Dumas
1952	Stella Alpine Rally	1	8V Zagato	O Capell
1954	3 Hours of Bari	1	As above	E Zagato

Competition Results

Year	Event	Result	Car	Driver(s)
1954	Coppa Intereuropa	1	As above	As above
1975	Giro d'Italia	1	Abarth SE031	G Pianta/B Scabini
Rallies:				
1972	Acropolis	1	124 Abarth Rally – 1756cc	H Lindberg/H Eisendle
	Poland	1	As above	A Warmbold/J Todt
1973	Acropolis	2	As above	R Aaltonen/R Turvey
1974	Portugal	1	As above	R Pinto/A Bernacchini
1975	Portugal	1	As above	M Alén/I Kivimaki
1976	1000 Lakes	1	131 Abarth Rally (Olio Fiat 131)	M Alén/I Kivimaki
1977	Portugal	1	As above	M Alén/I Kivimaki
	South Pacific (NZ)	1	As above	F Bachelli/F Rossetti
	Quebec	1	As above	T Salonen/J Markkula
	San Remo	1	As above	J-C Andruet/C Delferrier
	Tour de Corse	1	As above	B Darniche/A Mahé
	Fiat is World Rally Champion			
1978	Portugal	1	131 Abarth Rally (Alitalia)	M Alén/I Kivimaki
	Acropolis	1	As above	W Röhrl/C Geisdörfer
	1000 Lakes	1	As above	M Alén/I Kivimaki
	Quebec	1	As above	W Röhrl/C Geisdörfer
	Tour de Corse	1	As above	B Darniche/C Delferrier
	Fiat is World Rally Champion			
1979	1000 Lakes	1	As above	M Alén/I Kivimaki
1980	Monte Carlo	1	131 Abarth Rally (Fiat)	W Röhrl/C Geisdörfer
	Portugal	1	As above	W Röhrl/C Geisdörfer
	Argentina	1	As above	W Röhrl/C Geisdörfer
	1000 Lakes	1	As above	M Alén/I Kivimaki
	San Remo	1	As above	W Röhrl/C Geisdörfer
	Fiat is World Rally Champion			
1981	Portugal	1	As above	M Alén/I Kivimaki
	San Remo	1	As above	W Röhrl/C Geisdörfer
2006	European Rally Champions	1	Abarth Grande Punto IRC	Various

BIBLIOGRAPHY

John Blunsden, *Formula Junior*, Motor Racing Publications, 1999 (ISBN 0-9530721-5-0)

William Boddy, *The History of Brooklands Motor Course*, Grenville Publishing, 1957

Adriano Cimarosti, *The Complete History of Grand Prix Motor Racing*, Motor Racing Publications, 1990 (ISBN 0-947981-50-0)

Elvio Deganello and Arturo Rizzoli, *Abarth all the cars*, Giorgio Nada Editore, 2009 (ISBN 978-88-7911-464-6)

Editoriale Domus, *All The Fiats*, Domus, 1999 (ISBN 978-88-721227-0)

Chris Jones, *Road Race*, George Allen & Unwin Ltd, 1977 (ISBN 0-04-796045-00)

Karl Ludvigsen, *Italian Racing Red*, Ian Allen Publishing, 2008 (ISBN [13] 978-1 7110-3331-3)

TASO Mathieson, *Grand Prix Racing 1906-1914*, Connaisseur Automobile A.B., 1965

Lord Montagu of Beaulieu, *The Gordon Bennett Races*, Cassell & Company Ltd, 1963

Valerio Moretti, *Grand Prix Tripoli 1925 – 1940*, Automobilia, 1994 (ISBN 88-7960-056-7)

David Owen, *Targa Florio*, Foulis, 1979 (ISBN 0-85429-235-7)

Martin Pfundner, *Alpine Trials & Rallies*, Veloce Publishing 2005 (ISBN 1-904788-95-5)

Laurence Pomeroy, *The Grand Prix Car, 1906-1939*, Motor Racing Publications, 1949

Anthony Pritchard and Keith Davey, *Italian High-performance Cars*, George Allen and Unwin, 1967

Graham Robson, *Fiat Sports Cars from 1945 to X1/9*, Osprey Publishing Limited, 1984 (ISBN 0-85045-558-8)

Graham Robson, *Fiat 131 Abarth*, Veloce Publishing, 2008 (ISBN 978-1-787111-11-0)

Graham Robson, *Monte Carlo Rally – The Golden Age 1911-1980*, Herridge & Sons, 2007 (ISBN 978-1-906133-00-9)

Michael Sedgwick, *Fiat*, Arco Publishing, 1974 (ISBN 0-668-03306-1)

More from Veloce ...

Fiat entered rallying in 1970, with the aim of becoming World Rally Champion – and it was the 131 Abarth of 1976-1980 which made that possible. It soon began winning world rallies, and, in 1977, 1978 and 1980, the 'works' team also won the World Championship for Makes, paving the way for successors the Lancia Rally 037 and the Delta Integrale.

ISBN: 978-1-787111-11-0
Paperback • 19.5x21cm • 128 pages
• 100 colour and b&w pictures

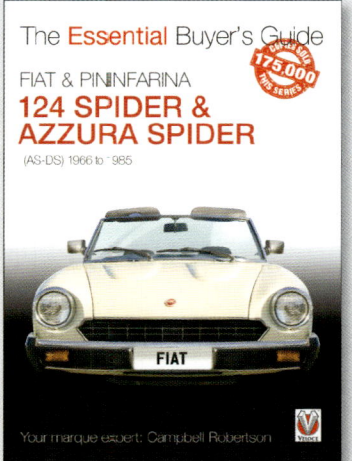

Having this book in your pocket is just like having a real marque expert by your side. Benefit from the author's years of 124 Spider ownership, learn how to spot a bad car quickly and how to assess a promising one like a professional. Get the right car at the right price!

ISBN: 978-1-787115-20-0
Paperback • 19.5x13.9cm • 96 pages
• 70 colour pictures

For more information and price details, visit our website at www.veloce.co.uk
email: info@veloce.co.uk • Tel: +44(0)1305 260068

Fiat & Abarth 124 Spider & Coupé covers the complete history of these important cars, including motorsport. Packed with expert advice on which model to choose, restoration, clubs, specialists and what it's like to live with a Fiat 124 Spider or Coupé.

ISBN: 978-1-845849-97-9
Paperback • 25x20.7cm
• 160 pages • 231 pictures

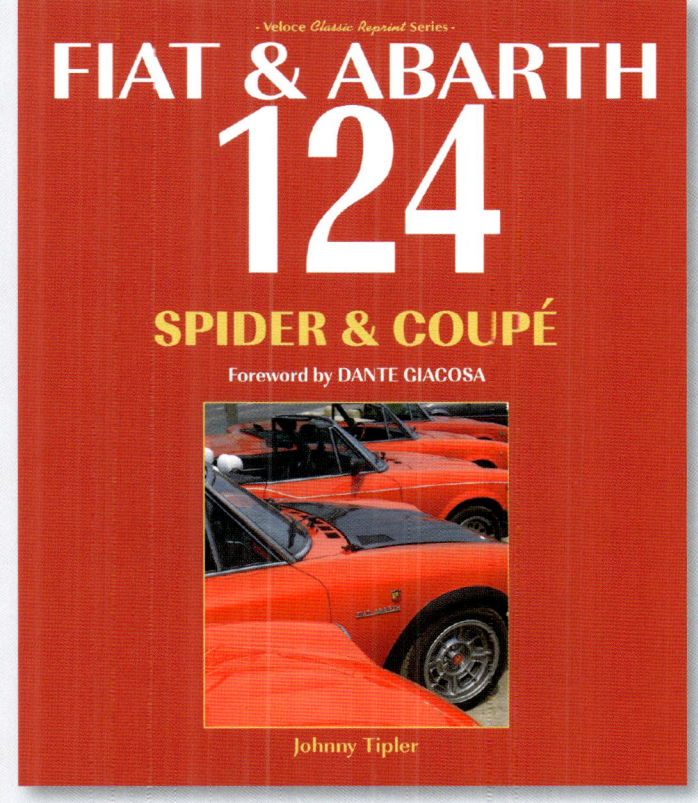

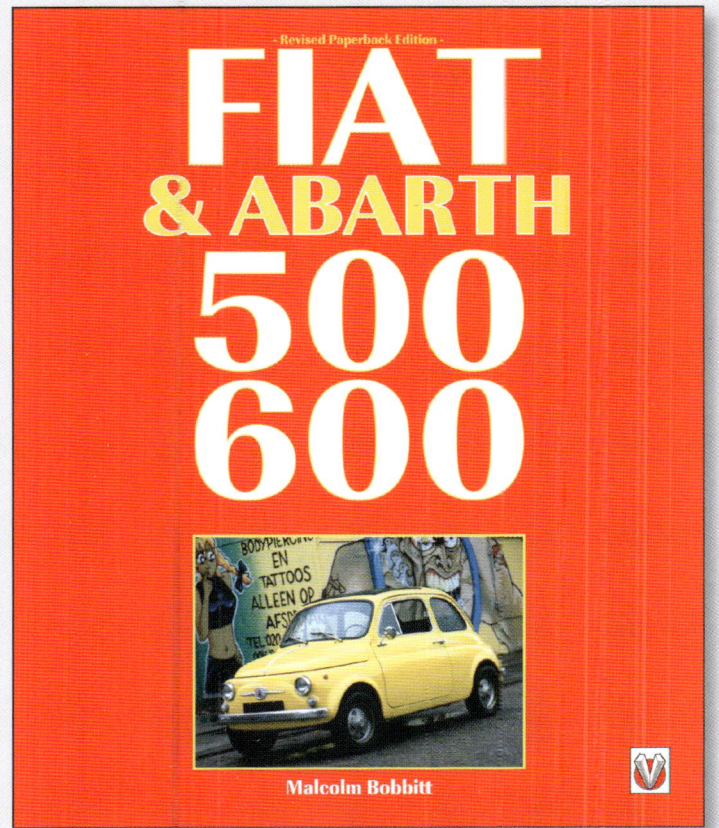

Fiat & Abarth 500 & 600 covers all the classic 'baby' Fiats, from the famous Topolino onwards: here is their full and eventful story.

ISBN: 978-1-845849-98-6
Paperback • 25x20.7cm
• 160 pages • 242 colour and b&w pictures

For more information and price details, visit our website at
www.veloce.co.uk
email: info@veloce.co.uk • Tel: +44(0)1305 260068

Index

Aaltonen, Rauno 114
Abarth 114
Abarth, Karl (Carlo) 142
Abarth models
   500 149
     750 Derivative 90, 91, 142
     A112 147
     Record breakers 144, 145, 147
     SE 031 120
Abercromby, Sir George 52
Agadir Crisis 21
Agnelli, Giovanni 7, 9, 10, 13, 60
Ahrens, Kurt, Jr 113
Alberti 106, 107
Alberti, Giovanni 107
Alboreto, Michele 148
Alén, Markku 114, 117, 123, 124, 126, 128, 131-135, 137-141
Ambrosini 63
Andruet, Jean-Claude 124, 128, 130, 134, 137-139
Angelini, Luigi 48
Angelvin, Dr M 90
Annus Mirabilis 21
Armstrong 90
Ascari, Antonio 46
Auricchio 83, 85
Auto Avia 815 77
Autobianchi 147

Bablot, Paul 64
Bacchelli, Fulvio 117, 118, 120, 124, 126, 128, 130
Bandini, Lorenzo 106, 110
Basagni 66
Bassi 78
Becchia, Walter 47
Benigni 60
Bergese, Tersilio 48, 49
Bertarelli 60
Bertarione, Vincenzo 47
Bettega, Attilio 137-141
Biagini 74
Bignan, Jacques 62, 64
Bira, B 81
Biscaretti di Ruffia, Count Roberto 7, 9
Bisulli, Giulio 117
Bonetto, Felice 79
Bordeu, Juan Manuel 106, 108, 109, 113
Bordino, Pietro 13, 32,36, 48, 49, 50, 54, 55, 58-60
Borsetto 14
Bosardé 26

Boschis 19, 32
Bragg, Caleb 33, 41, 42
Brambeck 44
Branca, Aquilino 108
Brault 89
Brendel 74
Brilli-Peri, Count Gaston 48-50
Brogliotti 48
Bruce-Brown, David 25, 33, 34, 39, 41
Businello, Roberto 106, 107

Cacherano di Brichesario, Count Emmanuele 7
Cagno, Alessandro 12, 14, 15, 17, 43, 44, 50, 59
Cales, Jacques 113
Cambiaghi 117
Cammarota, Raffaele 107-110
Capelli, Ovidio 75, 78, 83, 85
Capello, Dindo 149
Cappa, Cesare 47
Carini 91
Carpenter, Peter 110
Castelbarco 86
Casteldelli 58
Castiglioni 59
Castore 9
Cavalli, Carlo 47
Cecchi 49
Cedrino, Emanuele 17-19, 21, 23-25
Ceirano Giovanni Battista & C 7, 8, 10
Cerrato, Dario 140, 141
Chevrolet, Louis 18
Coatalen, Hérve 75
Colini 74
Colonna, Fabio 90
Comirato, Alberto 83
Conelli, Carlo 47
Cortese 88
Costa 66
Crivellari, Erasmo 106
Crivellari, Nino 107, 108

D'Orey, Fritz 109, 110
Darniche, Bernard 130, 134, 139
Davis, Colin 106, 107, 112, 113
De Filippis, Maria Teresa 106
De Maria 67
De Moraes 43
De Palma, Ralph 28, 31, 39, 41
De Sanctis, Lucien 83,105, 106
De Sauge 78
Delageneste 91

Di Liddo 66
Di Silvo 90
Dubac-Taine, Madame 68
Duff, John 53
Duray, Arthur 21, 36
Dusio, Piero 73, 75, 78

Edge, Selwyn 27
Eldridge, Ernest 52, 53
Enrico, Giovanni 9 29
European Rally Championship 141

Faccioli, Aristide 9, 10, 29
Faggi, Dino 90
Fagnano 43
Fassina, Tony 128
Ferrara, Albino 68
Ferrari 61
Fessia, Professor Antonio 75
Ffrench-Davis, FH 73
Fiat models
   3½ HP 7
   3A 58, 59
   6 HP Corsa (also 6/8 HP) 9, 10, 13
   10 HP 50
   12 HP Corsa 9, 10, 12, 13
   12/15 HP (Zero or Brevetti Type 1A) 31, 43
   15/20 HP (Brevetti) 23, 31
   16 HP 15
   18/24 HP 26
   20/30 Hp (Type 3) 44
   24 HP Corsa 11, 13, 14, 17, 19, 21, 23
   24/40 HP 19, 23
   28/40 HP Targa Florio Corsa 19, 21, 25, 28
   30/45 HP 44
   50/60 HP 31, 44
   60 HP Corsa 14, 15, 18, 27
   75 HP Corsa 13-15
   90 HP 15
   100 HP Corsa 15 17
   110 HP Gordon Bennett Corsa 16, 17, 21
   120 HP 23
   130 HP 21, 23
   500 (La Topolino) 75, 78, 83, 88, 91, 145
   501, 501 S, 501 SS 47-49, 59
   508, S (Balilla) 62, 67, 69, 72, 75
   508 C, CS, CMM 68, 74, 76, 78
   509, 509 A, S, SC 60-65, 67
   510 59
   514S, MM, CA 65–67
   519, 519S 55, 59, 61

   521, C, Siata 63
   522, C, L 66
   525 S 63, 66
   600 90
   801-401 47,48
   801-402 48, 49
   802 (or 501SS) 49
   803-403 49, 55
   804-404 48, 49, 60
   805-405 50, 54, 59, 60
   806-406 60
   1100 E 88-90
   1100 MM 76
   1100 S, ES 78, 82, 83
   1100-103, 103 TV 90
   1400 90
   1500 74-77, 82, 89
   2300S 147
   Cyclone 24
   Mephistopheles 52, 53
   SB 4 Corsa 27, 28, 50, 53
   S57/14B Corsa 43, 44, 47
   S57A/14B Corsa 48-50
   S61 & 61 Corsa 28, 31, 33, 41, 76
   S74 Corsa 33, 39, 42, 43
   S76 (Beast of Turin) 35, 36
   Taunus Corsa 22
   'Welleyes' 7, 9
   Fiat specials/etcetrinis:
   Bandini 92
   Cisitalia 73, 78, 89, 92
   Dagrada 92
   De Sanctis 95, 107, 110, 112
   Ermini 88, 90, 95
   Foglietti 96, 105
   Giaur/Giannini 88, 90, 96
   Gordini 75, 76, 97
   Moretti 98, 107
   Motto 98
   Nardi 98
   OSCA 97, 110, 112, 113
   Raineri 98, 105
   Raor 90
   Siata 75,77, 83, 88-90, 98
   Stanguellini 75, 77, 90, 91, 99, 105-113
   Taraschi 102, 105-107, 113
   Volpini 102, 105-107
   Wainer 104, 106, 113
   Gordini Fiats 72
   8V (Otto Vu) 85, 86, 88
   124 Sport Spider 114
   124 Abarth Rally 114, 117, 147
   125 114

131 (incl 'Mirafiore') 117, 120, 124,
  131 Abarth Rally 120, 126, 128, 130, 131, 134, 137, 138, 139, 140, 141, 148
  Abarth Grande Punto S2000 141
  Campagnola 89
  Ritmo 138, 139
  X1/9 118, 148
Filippini 44
Fiorio 83
Florio, Vincenzo 19, 26, 31
Fogolin 10, 14,
Fokin, Alexander 23, 26, 27
Formula Fiat Abarth 148
Formula Italia 148
Formula Junior 105
Fornaca, Guido 29, 47
Frescobaldi, Piero 106

Geneva Motor Show 83, 85, 90
Genovese, Carmelo 108
Ghia 85
Ghinzani, Piercarlo 148
Giaccone, Enrico 49, 50
Giacomelli, Bruno 148
Giacosa, Dante 75, 85
Gianotti 49
Gilera 63, 66-68
Giordano, Giuseppe 39, 43
Gordini, Amédée 69, 70, 72, 74
Goria-Gatti, Cesare 7, 9
Gosch 44
Grandsire, Henri 112
Grönholm, Ulf 135
Gropelli 65

Heal, Anthony 76
Hearne, Eddie 31
Heinz, Bino 109
Hémery, Victor 33
Hollander 14
Husem 68

Itala 8

Jano, Vittorio 47

Knapp, Jindrich 68
Kozma 74

Lampiano, Evasio 49
Lancia, Vincenzo 7, 9, 10, 13-15, 17-23, 25-28
Land speed record attempts
  Arpajon 53, 58
  Ostend 36
  Saltburn by the Sea 36
Lapinen, Simo 126, 128, 130-132
Leto di Priolo 85
Lettich, Dr Armand 66
Lippi, Roberto 105-107, 110
Lopez, Luigi 44
Lorenzelli, Livio 117, 128
Losa 67
Loyer, Roger 78, 79
Macchieraldo 81

Maglione, Antonio 106, 107, 110
Mäkinen, Timo 126, 130
Malaguti, Romano 74
Malaret, E 62
Manci 60
Mandrini 90
Manfredini, Corrado 106, 113
Manicatide, Dr 76
Manzon, Robert 78, 79
Maravigna, Pio 47
Marchesi, Enrico 7
Marchesio, Onesimo 54
Martens 70
Masetti, Count Giulio 46-48
Materassi, Emilio 47
Mathis, Emil 31, 32
May, Michael 106, 108-110, 112
Mazza 65
Michelet 78
Mikkola, Hannu 47
Miller 14
Minio, Ruggerio 69, 74
Minoia 46-48
Minozzi 61
Moalli 61
Morettini 74
Mouton, Michèle 130, 134, 137-139
Munari, Sandro 132-134, 137
Murray 62
Mussolini, Vittorio 74

Nannini, Alessandro 149
Napier 27
Narischkine, Prince L 68
Nazzaro, Biagio 49
Nazzaro, Felice 7, 9, 10, 12-14, 17-25, 27, 28, 32, 35, 49, 50, 52, 54, 55, 63, 66
Newton, Frank 27
Niccolini, Paolo 47-50
Nobile, Luigi 88, 105
Nuvolari, Tazio 78, 82

Ogna, Domenico 90
Okura, Kishichiro 23
Oldfield, Barney 42
Olympia Motor Show 23, 26

Paganelli, Alcide 114
Pagani 59
Paris Motor Show 90
Parker, Ed 24, 31
Pastore, Cesare 54, 55, 63
Patrese, Riccardo 148
Pellegrino, Giuseppe 48
Periccioli 65
Pianta, Giorgio 120
Piccolo 90
Pilloud 68
Pininfarina 83, 85
Pinto, Raffaelle 114
Piro, Giuseppe 47
Pirocchi, Renato 107, 110
Pirro, Emanuele 149
Pittaway, Duncan 39
Poillucci 85

Polensky, Helmut 90

Races/hillclimbs, etc
Albi Grand Prix 107
Alessandria 58
Aosta-St Bernard 86
Ards TT 72, 74
Atlanta 31, 32
Bari Three Hours 85
Belgian Ten Hours 68
Beverley Hills 48
Biella-Oropa 58
Bol d'Or 72, 74-76, 81
Bollinger Cup 32
Bologna-Corticella-P.Renatico-Malabergo-Bologna 9
Bombay 23
Boston 14
Boulogne 31
Brazil 28
Brescia 48
Brescia-Cremona-Mantua-Verona-Brescia (Florio Cup) 9, 15
Briarcliff Trophy 24
British Grand Prix 60
Brooklands 23, 27, 36, 52, 54, 74
Buenos Aires 32, 44
Caserta 107
Cape May 18
Casablanca 54
Cesanatico 106
Cincinnati 34
Circuito del Lido di Venezia 79
Circuito del Montenero 79
Circuit des Ardennes 14
Circuit des Ramparts 78, 79
Circuit d'Orleans 72
Circuito di Caracalla 79
Circuito di Vercelli 79
Circuito di Vigerano 79
Cologne-Trier-Cologne 59
Concosso Panrusso 59
Conegliano 13
Consuma Cup 14, 15, 46-48
Coppa Acerbo 58
Coppa Agnelli 61
Coppa Crespi 62
Coppa d'Oro 19
Coppa delle Cascine 48
Coppa delle Faucille 49
Coppa di Minneapolis 28
Coppa Fiera di Milano 59
Coppa Florio 28
Coppa Intereuropa 85
Coppa Internazionale di Monza 85
Coppa Mégevet 31
Coppa Sila 62
Coot-tha 50
Cortina 106
Coupe de la Commision Sportive 75, 76
Coupe de la Mediterranée 78
Coupe de Lyon 31
Coupe de Paris 79, 81
Coupe de Robert Benoist 79, 81
Coupe des Petite Cylindres 79, 81

County Down Trophy race 73
Croatia 43
Cuba 19, 34
Culver City 59
Czechoslovak 1000 mile race 68, 69
Daytona 15, 19
Delhi-Bombay 15
Eagle Rock 15
Eifel mountains 58
Eifel Pokal 109
Eifelrennen 74
Empire City 15, 18, 21
European Grand Prix 50
Eymountiers 74
Fanø 46
Feldberg 74
Fiat/Napier challenge 27
Figueras-Lisbon 13
Florence Cup 44
Frankfurt 31
French Grand Prix/Grand Prix de France 19, 23, 27, 33, 43, 49, 50, 54
Gallarate 47, 58
Geneva 35
Germany 60
Giro d'Italia 9, 13, 68, 118, 120
Giro dell'Umbria 85
Glacier Cup 63
Gordon Bennett Cup 12, 14-17
Gothenburg-Stockholm 19, 44,
Gran Premio di Milano 60
Gran Premio Luigi Arcangeli 79
Gran Premio Vetturette 49, 50
Grand Prix de Bourgogne 78
Grand Prix de Comminges 76
Grand Prix Monaco-Junior 106
Grand Prix of Turin 78
Grand Rapids 31
Grossglockner Hillclimb 73
Harmashatar Hillclimb 68, 74
Hartford 18
Havana Grand Prix 110
Herkomer Trophy 19
Hockenheim 78
Imperial Valley 43
Indianapolis 34, 41, 59
Italian Grand Prix 48, 49
Junior Cup 105
Kaiserpreis 22, 23
Klagenfurt 113
Klausen Hillclimb 68
Le Mans 68, 75, 76, 83, 89, 91
Lewes 67
Limone-Cuneo-Turin 9
Littorio races 75
Lorraine Grand Prix 73
Los Angeles 32, 34, 48
Los Angeles-New York 17
Los Angeles-Sacramento 43
Luton Hoo 28
Madunina Cup 110
Manx Cup 81
Mar del Plata 28, 32
Marchirez 31
Marne Grand Prix 72

Marseille 32
Messina 109
Milan 14, 18
Mille Miglia/Gran Premio delle Brescia 60, 62, 63, 65-68, 73-78, 82, 83, 85, 86, 88-90
Milwaukee 42
Minneapolis 31
Modena 105
Monaco 112
Mont Ventoux 17, 43, 64
Monte Pellegrino-Palermo 142
Montlhéry 106
Monza 106, 108
Monza Junior Cup 105, 113
Morris Park 18, 23
Moscow-Orel 32
Moscow-Twer 31
Mount Gugger 74
Mugello 49, 58
Narbeth 32
New York 18, 23, 24
Northway 48
Novgorod-Moscow 54
Nürburgring 108
Odessa 43
Oporto 105
Ormond Beach 15, 24
Oulton Park 110
Padua 12, 14
Padua-Bassano-Vincenza-Padua 9
Paris-Madrid 14
Parma-Poggio di Berceto 46-50
Pau 106
Penya Rhin Grand Prix 78
Pergusa 107
Pescara 113
Pescara 12 Hours 85
Piombino-Grosseto 12
Poland 60
Posillipo 106
Poughkeepsie 18
Prince Rainier Cup 75
Prix de Leman 81
Pyrnpass 44
Readville 14
Riunione di Modena 32
River Plate 58
Riverhead 31
Rocca di Papa 85
Romania 62
Rosario-Cordova 35
St Petersburg-Moscow 23, 26
St Petersburg-Sebastapol 35
Salerno 112, 113
Saluzzo 12
San Sebastian 28, 32
Santa Monica 41
Sassi-Superga 13, 78

Savannah-Grand Prize 28, 33
Semmering 22
Sofia 44
Solitude 109
Southport 14
Spa 74
Stelvio 60, 74
Stockholm 49
Susa-Moncenisio 13, 15, 17, 48, 75
Sydney-Mudgee-Singleton-Sydney 43
Syracuse 32, 110, 113
Tacoma 42
Targa Abruzzo 60, 62, 73, 75
Targa Acerbo 62
Targa Florio 19, 21, 23, 25, 27, 29, 31, 32, 39, 43, 44, 46-48, 55, 59, 62, 66-68, 74, 75, 77, 81, 83, 86, 88, 90
Tour de France 118
Tripoli Grand Prix (Circuit of Tripolitania) 58, 60, 63, 76
Turin-Asti 9
Turin-Chieri 9
Valencia 32
Valentino Park 78
Vallelunga 105-107, 110
Valparaiso 44
Vanderbilt Cup 15, 17, 18, 20, 28, 31, 42
Vercelli 43
Vigorelli Trophy 105
Villanova-Bologna 13
Vincenza-Padua 9
Radley, James 28
Rallies/raids
  Acropolis Rally 114, 126, 132, 134, 139, 140
  Algiers-Cape Town-Algiers Raid 89
  Alpine Cup Trial 44, 63, 66
  Arctic Rally 117
  Blackpool Rally 74
  Circuit des Vosges 68
  Circuit of the Carpthians 44
  Circuit of Ireland 137
  Coppa del Garda 59
  Coppa delle Tre Venezia 66
  Costa Brava Rally 114, 117
  Critérium du Québec 128, 132
  East African Coronation Safari Rally, East African Safari Rally, Safari Rally 90, 114, 134
  French Alpine Rally 78
  Freiburg-Travemünde Rally 90
  Island of Elba Rally/Elba Rally 114, 124
  Le Touquet Rally 64
  Liège-Brescia-Liège 91
  Monte Carlo Rally 62, 67, 68, 74, 76, 89, 114, 117, 124, 131, 134, 140, 147
  Moroccan Rally 62, 124
  New Zealand Rally 134, 139
  Paris-Nice Rally 75, 76

  Paris-St Raphael 68
  Polish Rally 90, 114
  RAC Rally 68, 74, 117, 130, 134, 137
  Rally Codasur 139
  Rally delle Valli Piacentine 120
  Rally 10,000 Trabucchi 120
  Rallye Côte d'Ivoire 133
  Rallye de France 139
  Rallye de Portugal 114, 117, 126, 132, 138, 140
  Rally delle Alpi Orientali 118
  Rally of 1000 Lakes 114, 124, 126, 132, 135, 139, 140
  San Remo Rally 114, 117, 124, 128, 133, 137, 139, 141
  South Pacific Rally 126
  Stella Alpine Rally 85
  Swedish Winter Cup Rally 117, 124, 131, 134, 138
  Torquay Rally 74
  Tour de Corse Rally 128, 134, 137
  Tulip Rally 90
  Viking Rally 90
Rapi, Fabio Luigi 35
Reutemann, Carlos 139
Revol, Robert 108
Riccioli, Eugenio 63
Röhrl, Walter 128, 131, 132, 134, 137-139
Rol 90
Russo, Giacomo ('Geki') 110

Saden 50
Salamano, Carlo 50, 63, 78
Salmson, Emil 19, 21, 23
Salonen, Timo 128, 131-133, 137
Samsing 90
Sartori, Paul 15
Savicki 44
Savio 76
Savonuzzi, Giovanni 142
Scales, Jack 43
Scampini, Elio 58
Scarfiotti, Ludovico 86, 90
Schell, Harry 79
Schott 14
Schudt 32
Sciandra 67
Scuderia Ambrosiana 75
Scuderia Madunina 105, 106
Siata 66, 67
Sigrand 91
Silvani 61
Simca 72, 78
Sivocci, Ugo 48
Società Ceirano Automobili Torino (SCAT) 8
Sommer, Raymond 79
Soukhanoff, Boris 35, 36, 39
Sozzi, Carlo 47
Stanguellini, Vittorio 76

Stjernsvaerd 49
Storero, Luigi 12-15, 17
Stothert 68, 74
Strang, Lewis 31
Stuck, Hans 78
Sullivan, Billie 74

Tamburi 63
Tarabusi, Augusto 48, 58
Taruffi, Piero 76, 79, 81
Tett 74
Tetzlaff, Teddy 41, 42
Thiele, Alfonso 90
Tinazzo, Alfredo 106-108
Toia, Francesco 68
Toivonen, Henri 135
Trivero, Alberto 58, 60
Tuson, V.H. 76

Ulyate, Robin 114

Verbeck, Frank 43
Verini, Maurizio 114, 117, 126, 128, 130, 131, 133
Viale 75
Vignale 85
Villoresi brothers 68
Villoresi, Luigi 73, 74
Vinatier, Jean 133
Vincent, Francis 130
Viotti 74, 75
Von Trips, "Taffy" 108, 109
Vudafieri, Adartico 141

Wagner, Louis 20, 23, 26-28, 33, 39, 48
Waldegard, Björn 138
Wallace, William 15
Walter Junior 68
Warmbold, Achim 114
Weber, Eduardo 44, 48
Weillschott, Dr Aldo 20, 21
Westwood 74
Wimille, Jean-Pierre 81
Witkowski 90
Woodhead 50
World Rally Championship for Drivers/FIA Cup for Drivers 130, 133, 134, 140
World Rally Championship for Manufacturers 130, 134, 137, 140, 147

Zaitti 63
Zanarotti, Alberti 107, 108, 110
Zanarotti, Gastone 106, 107
Zanelli, Antonio 62
Zagato 85
Zagato, Elio 85, 86
Zannini, Luigi 105, 106
Zerbi, Tranquilo 47